Building the PT Boats

Frank J. Andruss, Sr.

NIMBLE BOOKS LLC

NIMBLE BOOKS LLC

Nimble Books LLC

1521 Martha Avenue

Ann Arbor, MI, USA 48103

http://www.NimbleBooks.com

wfz@nimblebooks.com

+1.734-330-2593

Copyright 2009 Frank J. Andruss, Sr.

Version 1.0; last saved 2009-05-18.

Printed in the United States of America

ISBN-13: 978-1-608880-73-7

ISBN-10: 1-934840-85-8

Photo and Documentation Credits: National Archives, Andrew Shannahan, Electric Boat Company, Huckins Yacht Corporation, Alex Johnson, PT Boats Incorporated, Ed Behney, Navy War College Museum, R. Perry Collins, Cindy Purcell, Jerry E. Strahan, Bruce Marshall, Rick Grant, Capt. Robert J. Bulkley Jr., T. Garth Connelly, U.S. Naval Institute.

Contents

FOREWORD

When I was asked to write the foreword for this book, I was both surprised and honored to do so. Early in October 1942, our Squadron Three PT boats arrived off Guadalcanal. We had eight Elco 77-foot boats and they were splendid. Perched on boats made of many types of wood, we met the enemy head on, although his ships were made of steel. I remember being armed with the Mk 8 Torpedo in four black, powder charged tubes. Two sets of fifty-calibre machine guns rounded out our armament. Our boats were powered with three Packard V-12 engines, which gave us speed we desperately needed to survive.

Many nights our boats, struggling from a lack of spare parts, continued to perform, as we roared out to do battle in an area known as Iron Bottom Sound. Our primary missions were to halt the bombardment of Henderson Field, and stop the Japanese from supplying Guadalcanal with troops and supplies. The Japanese would send several destroyers on these fast missions, which we called the Tokyo Express. We had neither the sea power nor the air power to counter all these thrusts.

The Navy felt that our PT boats could do the job of disrupting the Japanese. Built for speed and torpedo attacks, our boats performed wonderfully. We often moved in with engines muffled, trying to line up a destroyer to launch our "fish." Many times we were detected before we could perform our mission and wound up running for our very lives and depending on our boats to see us through. The PT boat performed like a greyhound racing for the long haul, staying ahead of the Japanese Destroyers, which were very fast themselves. Because the PT boats drew only four feet of water, we could get in close to shore, and lose the destroyers.

I remember one night being chased by a destroyer in *PT-48* and beaching the boat to prevent it from being destroyed.

Although our total hits on Japanese shipping during the Guadalcanal campaign has been downplayed by historians, there is no doubt that our PT boats wrecked havoc with the enemy. While skipper of *PT-45*, we were credited with the sinking of the new Japanese destroyer, *Terutsuki,* along with Stilly Taylor and Williams Kreiner. This was Admiral Tanaka's flagship, who was injured in the blast and removed from the ship. My service in the Guadalcanal area lasted about one year, in which I used only the 77-foot Elco boats. I found the boats were able to withstand all types of weather, and still continue to perform.

I was assigned as an instructor at the Motor Torpedo Boats Squadrons Training Center at Melville, RI, after my stint in Guadalcanal. I had the chance to pilot both the Higgins PT boats and the Huckins boats while at the Training Center. Both were very good boats that I found to be equally good as the Elco. The Higgins boats could really maneuver well. I was assigned as a Lt. Commander with Squadron 26 to the Hawaiian Sea Frontier, where we had no less than ten Huckins PT boats. Huckins boats were without a doubt the smoothest riding PT's we had. My biggest thrill came when I was asked to take a group of Navy brass to the Elco Naval Division in Bayonne, NJ. It was a rough and stormy ride and all on board except me was seasick. I arrived at the plant and was taken through the buildings to see just how these great boats were made. I remember seeing all those workers crowding the hulls like a group of angry bees, each one performing their task at hand. They worked and built these boats with infinite care.

I was happy that I was on an Elco PT boat while in combat, and I now know that because of the workers at Elco, my life was saved many times because of the boat's ability to get in quick, lay smoke and get out before the enemy could train his guns on us. Yes, these boats are etched in my mind some 60 years later, and I can only thank those who worked so hard to build our PT fleet into the most feared, small, fast, wooden fighting boats the world will ever know..."

Lt. Cmdr. Lester H. Gamble
Squadrons 3 & 26

PREFACE

This is my first attempt at trying to produce a book. I do not pretend to be an author, but they say you have to have some type of title so people can identify you. So be it. My goal is to try and keep your attention in photographs. I have always felt that people enjoy looking at pictures because it captures the imagination and freezes time for future generations to enjoy. I decided to work on this project for several reasons. I guess the first would be my love for PT boats. It was a picture of a PT boat that captured my eyes as a ten year old in 1967. Gliding through the waves like a playful dolphin, only with much more power, the boat seemed to leap from the photograph. I was amazed as I saw the frothy foam that was produced by those three Packard marine engines. The boat looked long and sleek and reminded me of a greyhound trying to catch up with that blasted rabbit, so it could deliver the fatal bite.

I closed my eyes and tried to imagine what it was like to go zipping across the ocean on this fast, wooden, boat. Years have gone by since I first saw that photo, but to tell you the truth, I never lost that deep feeling for these boats. I can still see myself at the wheel, closing the enemy somewhere in the Pacific. The Electric Launch Company (Elco) was the front runner in wooden boat building, so it was fitting that during World War Two, they mass produced more PT boats than any other company. The other reason I decided to write this book was that there is not enough media that focuses on the men and women who produced these boats. Working side by side, workers pitched in to help build Uncle Sam's fighting PT boats, often working long, hard, hours.

This pictorial look of the building of these wonderful boats, will take you back to a time when wooden designed PT boats were made with pride and rushed to the war front. You will get an inside look at three major Companies that were awarded contracts to build Uncle Sam's PT fleet, Elco Naval Division, Higgins Industries, and Huckins Yacht Corporation. It should be noted that Huckins is still in business after 70 years. I hope to show you everyday life of the common worker as he/she came to work each day. To dedicate this book to these workers is an understatement. I hope that this book will reach the small majority of those who worked there, so that it might jog their memory and bring them back to a time when people came together for one common cause; freedom. To others who view this book, I hope you too will get a sense of what it must have been like to build these wonderful wooden boats. Although the PT boats have long been retired, the people who built them will forever be a part of naval history.

ACKNOWLEDGEMENTS

So many people were very supportive of this project that I must extend my thanks to them. First, to my wonderful wife, Stacia, who for the past thirty plus years had to listen to my endless stories about PT boats. She has been my inspiration in everything I do in my life, and without her I am lost. To my Mom and Dad, who taught me from an early age that anything is possible if you work hard. To my many friends who served on PT boats during World War Two, you were the Knights of the Sea. To the best two sisters God ever created (Lori & Debbie). To Executive V.P. of PT Boats Inc., Alyce Guthrie, who without her help and resources, this book would not be possible. To Cindy Purcell, granddaughter of the late Frank P. Huckins, who opened her resources so that Huckins PT Boats could take their place in History. To Bruce Marshall for his tireless efforts and the Family of Irwin Chase Sr., your help was instrumental. Finally, a special thanks to those men and women who worked many long and tireless hours producing America's PT boats.

z

ELECTRIC LAUNCH COMPANY

The Electric Launch Company, or Elco, was founded in 1892. It was one of the pioneers in the boat building industry, a company that had the vision to discern the possibilities that boats offered for recreation and sport; the foresight to anticipate the changes that would be required both in building methods and in marketing; and the skill to create and to meet the demand for safe, seaworthy, and usable boats for those who wanted to get afloat for pleasure.

Early advertisements claimed that their boats had all the comfort of a summer cottage *piazza* and could be operated by a lady. Other articles over the years claimed that Elco launches couldn't explode, sink, or tip over. This was a time when the power and convenience of electric motors, vapor, and gasoline engines were attracting people to the water who previously knew little about boats of any kind.

The Electric Launch Company, which became the Elco Yacht and Naval Divisions of the Electric Boat Company, launched its first boat in 1892. During all the subsequent years, Elco played a leading role in bringing pleasure boating to its present popularity and degree of safety. It is safe to say that the cruisers and power yachts of America's boat builders today are the world's finest because of Elco. When the Elco Company entered the pleasure boat field, electricity for propulsive purposes was comparatively new and the internal combustion engine, especially for marine power use, was in its infancy.

Elco's engineers and designers saw the possibilities in both types of power. In 1893, at Chicago's first World Fair, electricity was the wonder of the age. Floating on the fair's lagoons were fifty-five electric boat launches, the first products of the Electric Launch Company. The general public was amazed and thrilled by these noiseless, smokeless, magically propelled craft. For the next seven years the company was kept busy with duplicate orders. Henry Ford, John Jacob Astor, and Mrs. W.K. Vanderbuilt were among their owners. Even the Czar of Russia, envious of Mr. Astor's luxurious launch, ordered a still finer one.

The company's first plant was located at Morris Heights, on the Harlem River, but by 1900 the demand for the boats had outgrown the facilities there and a new site was selected on Newark Bay in Bayonne, New Jersey. Elco remained at this location until 1949. The move to New Jersey was significant for another reason. In its new home, the company began to experiment with adapting gasoline engines to marine use, with results that are apparent to all those who have followed the development of power driven craft.

It was in 1904 that the first National Motor Boat Show was held in New York's old Madison Square Garden. Elco made this a memorable occasion by exhibiting, for the first time, the Auto Boat, the forerunner of the modern high-speed runabout. The company exhibited its cruisers in every boat show except in 1919 when no show was held on the account of the First World War.

Also, in 1904, Elco began an even more important project. For the United States Life Saving Service, now a part of the United States Coast Guard, the company developed the first self-righting, self-bailing, non-sinkable power lifeboat.

Hundreds were built and the basic principles and design are still in use today. The Coast Guard was not the only government service to make use of Elco designs. In 1907, the United States Revenue Service commissioned the company the build the first gasoline cutter. A year later, the United States Army ordered the impressive number of one hundred and twenty 20' workboats and thirty-two 32' mine laying motor boats. Elco designers did not specialize in government contracts alone, but brought about important developments in the private boat field as well. Veteran yachtsmen with long memories may recall that the world's first diesel motor yacht was the 84' *Idealia*. They may not readily remember that she was built in 1911 by Elco, not on order, but as a company sponsored experiment in this new field.

Sensing the potentialities of the pleasure boat field, Elco decided, in 1906, to establish a permanent design and engineering department. Staffed with experienced naval architects and marine engineers, Elco was the front runner for departments in all large manufacturing plants for other boat building companies. The demand for higher speeds and the popularity of speed boat racing offered a fruitful field for experiment and, in 1912, Elco designers adopted the hull design that made one hundred mile per hour racers possible in the 1940's. The stepped hydroplane-bottom was incorporated in the Elco-plane. One of these boats, the *Bug*, is said to have won $5,000 in a trail race against Frank J. Gould's 18 mph steam yacht *Helenita,* developing an average speed of 30mph over a course between Hunnington Bay and New London.

A pioneer in standardized construction as a means of greater economy of production, Elco made practical use of this idea in 1914 with the development of the Elco Cruisette, which was a double-cabin cruiser 32' in length. She was considered by yachtsmen and sailors as one of the best small cruising boats that had yet been built. As the years went by, this first Cruisette design became a fleet of pleasure craft of many lengths and designs for every purpose.

The original model was ruggedly seaworthy, as many manufactured boats of those days were not, and built of fine materials. She set a standard for the times. But that was just the beginning. Over the years, Elco's fleet of motor driven cruisers would offer luxury, beauty, and efficiency unknown in 1914.

It was during the First World War that Elco showed what a well-equipped plant and an efficient staff could do in the matter of quantity production and speed in producing small boats for the government and the Navies of the Allies. The German submarine was a grave menace to the Allied supply lines. The British Navy had to have quickly a vast fleet of fast, light, vessels capable of combating the menace. In this emergency, the British Admiralty and later the French, Italian, and American governments, placed contracts with Elco for large numbers of boats of the same design.

Elco met the emergency by designing a fast, seaworthy, submarine chaser and then achieved the amazing record of building 722 of these craft, 550 of them (known as the MLS) being turned out in the unbelievable time of 488 working days. This was all the more noteworthy because up to that time, no plant in the world had produced boats in any such quantity.

Elco had pioneered not only a new naval weapon in this small chaser, but also a new method of mass construction and, in doing so, played a major part in winning gone of the biggest battles of the last year of the war.

Thus it was the World War emergency that brought about the application of modified production line methods to the building of motor boats, a technique which Elco had developed to meet its huge naval orders. During the prosperous 1920's and the depressing 1930's, the company built literally thousands of motor yachts and cruisers for the fast growing yachting public. They were standardized in design and construction but they retained, in the craftsmanship with which they were fashioned and the quality materials used in them, the best elements of custom built craft.

This contribution to the war effort in 1914-18 and the incorporation of facilities for standardized production on a large scale placed the company in position to play an important part in the small boat building program of this government inaugurated after the fall of France in 1940, or even before the event occurred.

Already, the new Motor Torpedo Boats (PT's, or craft of the Patrol Torpedo type, as the U.S. Navy called them), built in the company's new plant at Bayonne, NJ, were in action in the Pacific and in the English Channel, and Elco was the first company to deliver fleets of these little giant killers to the United States Navy.

During World War Two, officers of the company realized that the boat building facilities in the United States, including those of the Elco plant itself, would not be able to meet the demands that would be put upon them. Plans were immediately made for expansion.

Next to the Elco Yacht Works, the company constructed a million dollar plant especially designed for Torpedo Boat building, one of the most complete building plants in the world for this type of wooden construction. It was erected in the astonishing time of only one hundred working days.

In this new Naval Division, there was assembled, under one roof, complete manufacturing facilities for building Motor Torpedo boats on a production line basis. This modern factory had machine shops, pipe fitting and bending shops, engine shops, boat building and joiner shops, as well as storage and stock rooms, etc. Outside was a special marine basin, complete with fitting out slips and a new type of launching crane which could handle boats in and out of the water at remarkable speed.

Due to its highly technical design and complicated construction, made necessary to obtain maximum strength for minimum weight to attain extremely high speed, building these fast wooden fighters presented more difficult problems than ordinary boat building. New shop layouts and new methods were necessary. The new Elco Naval Division plant provided and thus made possible the rapid turning out of boats. Roughly 399 Elco PT boats were produced during the War years in three different designs. First were the 70' Scott-Paine designed boats, made of double planked mahogany. This light weight boat was easy to plane and was of British design. Purchased by Elco's Executive Vice President, Henry R. Sutphen, he made arrangements to obtain American manufacturing rights. This Scott-Paine designed boat would be known as *PV-70* and a purchasing contract was signed by the Navy on June 1, 1939. The boat would make its wasy to New York as deck cargo aboard the liner SS President Roosevelt on September 5, 1939.

Here she would make her way to the Electric Boat Company (Elco) plant in Groton, Connecticut. Mr. Scott-Paine himself demonstrated the boat for a Navy trial board, along with Elco's Managing Constructor Irwin R. Chase. This 70 foot designed boat would later be painted and designated as *PT-9*, and impressed the trial board for its durability and speed. Weighing in at thirty tons, *PT-9* was lighter than most torpedo boats in service at that time. She was powered by three 1,100 hp Rolls-Royce Merlin engines converted for marine use. Her top speed with a full war load was a sustained 40 knots and she carried four eighteen-inch torpedoes. On the trunk cabin, further aft, she carried two Dewandre .50 caliber machine gun powered turrets that were covered by acrylic glass domes. The armament of this boat set the standard for the weapons layout of all pre-war American PT boats. Elco signed a contract with the Navy to build twenty-three seventy foot boats based on the Scott-Paine design. Elco's designed boats were numbered *PT-10* to *PT-19* and had some major differences from the Scott-Paine boat seen at the deck level and above. The Merlin engines were replaced with three 1,200 hp Packard marine engines. These engines became the standard power plants of all American PT boats. The pilot house in the forward section was enlarged and flushed with a trunk canopy, and so was the bridge. Aluminum grab rails were installed, and the .50-calibre gun tubes were also enlarged. Six cowl vents were installed on the aft portion of the deck. These boats never saw service with the US Navy, as they were turned over to the British under Lend-Lease. They saw considerable service with the 10th MTB Flotilla, being renumbered *MTBs 259* through *268*. Seeing the need to carry a larger torpedo, Elco's second class of boats were the 77 footers numbered *PTs 20* to *44*.

Even though it looked like someone just added seven feet to a seventy foot boat, they were actually a totally new design. The reverse sheer of the hull was not as pronounced as it had been, and the distance between the cowl vents on the stern also showed the new length to good advantage. Considerable strengthening of the hull could be seen below decks and intermediate framing was added in the forward section in the pounding area.

Standard issue Mark XVIII torpedo tubes were added to carry the Mark VIII twenty-one inch torpedoes. The Dewandre-turrets were replaced with the newer and simpler Elco turret design. Depression rails were also added to the turrets to keep gunners from shooting into their own boat. On the bow, a pair of .30-calibre Lewis machine guns on pedestal mounts were installed on either side of the pilot house, just forward of the pilot house superstructure. In May of 1941, the Navy held a trial to determine what types of boats would be chosen for the construction programs included within a fifty million dollar appropriation for the 1941 fiscal year. It was determined after these sea trials that the Elco boat was the fastest and had the driest ride of the other boats in the trials. Production started at Elco and it was these boats that first saw action against the Japanese at Pearl Harbor on December 7, 1941. Twelve of these boats made up Squadron One at Pearl Harbor, with *PTs 20* to *25* tied up at the submarine base when the Japanese attacked. *PTs 26* to *30* and *PT-42* were being readied for transport to the Philippines. *PTs 31, 32, 33, 34,35,* and *41* first saw action against the Japanese in the Philippines as Squadron 3 based at Cavite Navy Yard. These little giant sluggers met the enemy head on, proving that small PT Boats could do a good job in the shallow waters of the Pacific.

Later, *PT-41* rescued General Douglas MacArthur from the invading Japanese forces. Already the Navy was looking for a larger boat, and before the war began, plans were underway to have Elco switch production of these boats to the 80 foot design, while Elco still had to build and deliver twenty of the smaller boats that the contract had called for. Elco's last class of PT boats was a totally new design. It drew on the experience that Elco had achieved from its two earlier designs. Three feet bigger, this new 80 foot boat was the heaviest of all, at thirty-eight tons. Although slightly slower than and not as maneuverable as the *PT-20* class boat, they certainly had better sea keeping qualities. They were much better riding boats and could carry a larger warload. They were also much stronger than the 77 footer.

The crew accommodations on board the new Elco's were very well designed and had almost everything that the crew needed to stay aboard. Deckhouses were covered in marine plywood and hatches were installed for easier removal of the gas tanks and the three Packard engines. These boats were designed strictly for the fast torpedo boat role, and their armament layout was also changed. One twin .50 calibre machine gun turret was located on the starboard side of the cockpit and one on the portside of the aft dayroom cabin structure, approximately located amidships. A single 20 mm anti-aircraft cannon was mounted on the after deck. Four 21-inch torpedoes mounted in heavy steel tubes were mounted, two on either side of the boat. *PT-103*, laid down in January of 1942, was the first 80 foot boat built at Elco. It was completed on May 16, 1942 and at a ceremony was lowered into the basin.

During the war, this class underwent many changes, including removal of the heavy torpedo tubes, the addition of more weapons, the addition of better torpedoes, and increased horsepower. Radar was installed and gave the boats the edge they needed in night fighting It would become the most powerful and heaviest armed Elco of the war from 1942 to 1945, Elco turned out a total of three hundred twenty-seven of the eighty foot design. .. Elco was the front runner in PT boat design during the war, but would find things tough going after the conflict.

Heading back into the pleasure boat business, they were hard pressed to stay in business. Maintenance and upkeep of the once state-of-the-art boat building facility became a large overhead expense. Wood had become very expensive, and Elco refused to buy cheaper materials to make their boats. In 1946, Elco developed, designed, built, and tested five new model pleasure boats,; they settled all terminated War contracts, and received contract and design for two experimental PT boats. Elco also got into the car industry, building wood auto parts for Dodge and Plymouth, and developed plastic molded auto roofs. Elco even started building wooden bowling pins. They built up Elco Boat Dealer organizations of eighteen substantial dealers nationally distributed. What hurt Elco was their slowness in building up the working force. They had great difficulty in obtaining men during the summer and fall. Another problem was the difficulty in obtaining raw and fabricated materials due to employee strikes, and Government control. There were delays in perfecting details or designs, and re-conversion of the plant for commercial work was very slow. Establishing new costs for the pleasure boats was found to be considerably higher then their major competition.

In spite of these higher prices, Elco received widespread approval from dealers and retail buyers, and booked over two million dollars in orders. Elco steadily lost business during 1948, with other boat companies buying cheaper materials and Elco having delays in delivery. A letter dated April 15, 1948 from Preston L. Sutphen, Vice President and General Manager of Elco, simply stated that in view of the estimated loss for 1948 and the probable losses in 1949, he believed the Board of Directors should give careful consideration to closing out the Elco business and disposing of the plant. This historical place, that had produced more than 4,028 boats from 1915 to 1947, finally closed its doors for good in 1949.

Figure 1. *PT-10* sits proudly in front of building 21, the main assembly plant for the Elco Naval Division. She was Elco's first PT boat design; ten were constructed. Testing and trials were in Florida and Caribbean waters in the winter of 1940/41. Later these ten boats would be shipped to the British under the Lend Lease program, as they were considered too small for the U.S. Navy. (Author's collection)

Figure 2. Construction has begun on the concrete apron and roadway in front of building 21. Hundreds of yards of concrete were mixed and brought over using trucks. Laborers using wheelbarrows poured the concrete and others smoothed out the mix. Re-rod made of metal was placed in between the forms so that the concrete would not split or crack under the tremendous weight of the boats placed here. (Author's collection)

Figure 3. A look at the massive plant that became building 21. This PT boat assembly building cost one million dollars by the time it was completed on March 16, 1940. The building included machine shops, tool cribs, boat assembly, office space, joiner shops, and many other areas, making it a state-of-the-art boat building facility. The Elco Naval Division of the Electric Boat Company was one of only a handful of boat plants that were operational when the United States entered World War Two. (Author's collection)

Figure 4. Construction has begun on the large outdoor boat shed. This barge crane will lift the heavy steel girders into place. When completed, the shed will hold several PT boats, where other areas of assembly and trouble shooting can continue. A roof will be installed so workers can perform their tasks out of the elements. Boats running time trials out in Newark Bay will operate from this shed. Engine dockside trials will also be done in this area, and will free up much needed space in the basin. (Author's collection)

Figure 5. Building 21 is entering its final stages of construction. Here a steamroller is smoothing out the concrete roadway. The backside of this building will later be designated Building 20, where the offices of the U.S. Navy and the Office of Sup Ships will be located. Tons of concrete will be mixed and poured before the building is completed. The Elco site in Bayonne, New Jersey will ultimately include up to nineteen buildings, including construction buildings, storage areas, spray shops, a power house, lunch room, milling building, wet boat basin, Electro Dynamic Works, dipping building, metal shop, the Elco Yacht building, and even a vault. (Author's collection)

Figure 6. This photo shows the back side of Building 20. Notice the cradles used for the boats as they make their way to assembly areas. The boats are launched while attached to these heavy cradles, and then floated off in the basin. To the right is a steam shovel that is digging out a section of land. This area would later become the Elco athletic field, used for baseball and softball. Employees would have competitive teams in other sports such as bowling and soccer. (Ed Behney)

Figure 7. A wonderful aerial look at the Elco Complex in Bayonne, New Jersey. Many
buildings made up this complex during the war years. To the far left is building 21,
the main assembly plant for all PT Boats. In front of the plant is the large outdoor
boat shed. Notice the boat basin in front of the concrete roadway and the Elco
Crane on the dock. These breakwater pylons were important in keeping in keeping
calm water in the basins. You can also see the wet boat basin (center group of
buildings) and Elco's Yacht Division building (writing on roof). The large set of
buildings at the very back of the complex are the Electro Dynamics Works Company.
Most of these buildings, except building 21, were later destroyed in the great fire
that swept this area in 1963. (PT Boats, Inc. Germantown, Tennessee)

Figure 8. *PV-70,* named for Private Venture, is the British Scott-Paine designed boat. This boat was purchased by Elco under the direction of Elco's Executive Vice President, Henry R. Sutphen, and Chief Designer Irwin R. Chase (seen in cockpit). The boat's durability and speed impressed both Chase and Sutphen. (Author's collection)

Figure 9. Another look at *PV-70* as she produces a tremendous wake from her three powerful engines. She carries four 18 inch torpedoes. This boat made its way to New York as deck cargo on board the *SS President Roosevelt,* arriving September 5, 1939. From there she was lightered to the Electric Boat Company in Groton, Connecticut, opposite New London. There the boat was demonstrated for a Navy trial board. (Author's collection)

Figure 10. *PV-70* shows her low profile as she makes a head on pass. Notice the high bow which when at top speed would simply plane out of the water. Because of the boats light weight, planing was accomplished more easily. The chine, which curved up only slightly at the bow provided lift and spray rails located at the chine, just above the waterline, forced the bow wave beneath the boat. Managing Constructor of the Elco Naval Division, Irwin Chase is at the helm. He was instrumental in helping to create the stepless planning hull years before. (Author's collection)

Figure 11. *PV-70* has now been brought into the factory, where it will be completely
dismantled. Piece by piece, engineers and other workers will measure and remake
blueprints that did not come with the boat. In essence, Elco will start from scratch
before building these seventy foot boats. Here we see the engine room of *PV-70,*
still sporting the Rolls-Royce Merlin Engines. These will be replaced with the 4M-
2500 Packard Marine Supercharged Gasoline Engines. (Author's collection)

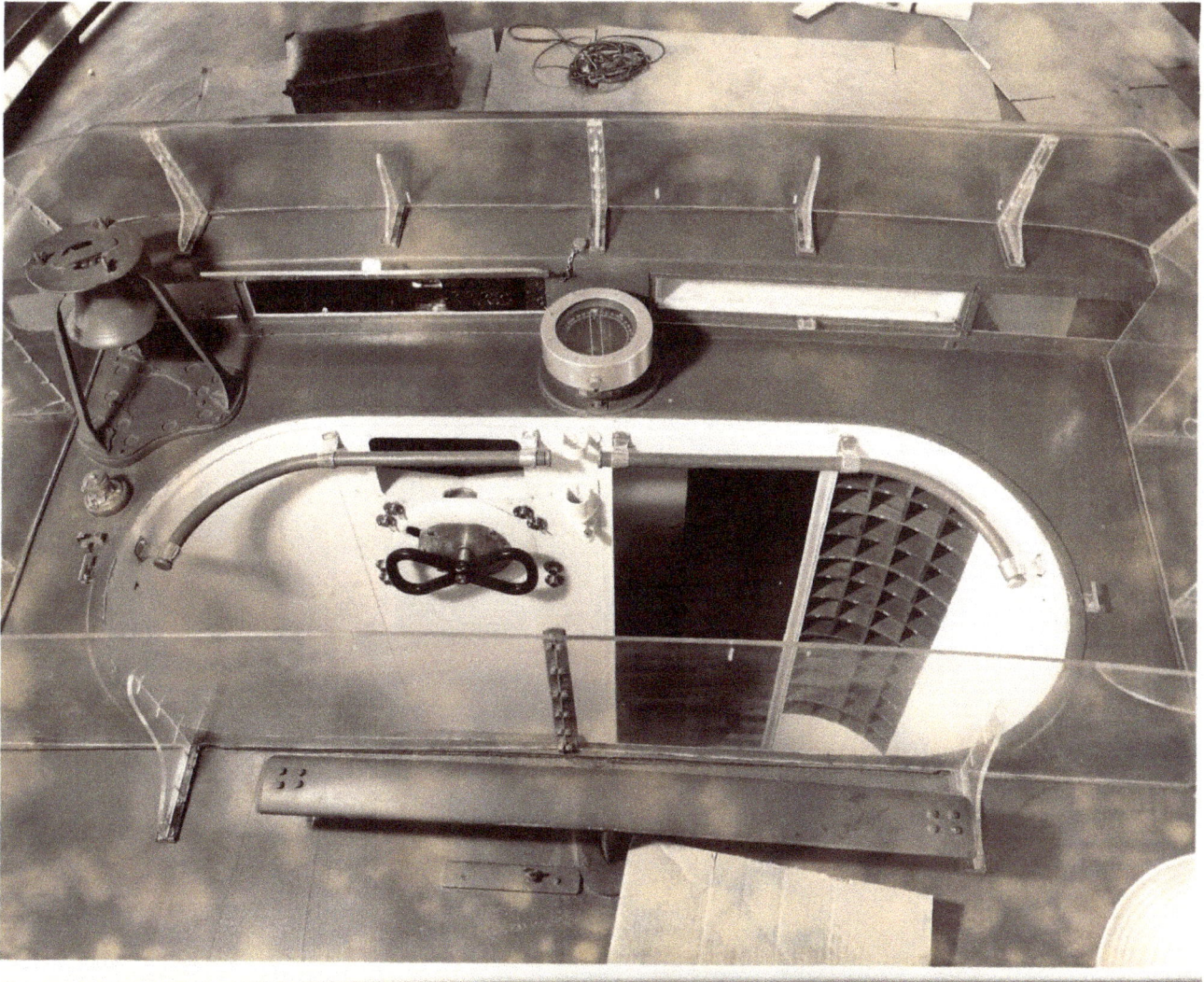

Figure 12. Notice the very small helm area of *PV-70*. Cockpit details show a companion way leading to the wheelhouse. Also shown is the small British-designed helm wheel and simple controls mimicking the duplicate controls found in the wheelhouse cabin. A searchlight combination boat bell mount can be seen in the upper left of the cockpit, although the searchlight has been removed. Directly behind the searchlight/bell mount is a covered electrical connector, which provides power to the searchlight when installed on top of the mount. On the cockpit's centerline, a heavy duty compass binnacle can be see as well as a complete PLEXIGLAS® type wrap around windscreen. Notice directly behind the rear PLEXISGLAS screen is the boat's telescoping mast in the lowered position. (Author's collection)

Figure 13. A detailed photo of *PV-70's* wheelhouse that was the basic model for Elco's first PT boat designs. Notice the boot that is attached to the lower front of the wheelhouse, which contains two hatches. This area was used for storage of deck items on the first Elco seventy-foot designs, and on most of the seventy-seven-foot designs as well. On the early seventy-seven-foot boats, these hatches seved double duty as ready boxes for forward-mounted machine guns. Elco Engineers were kept very busy as many drawings and blue-prints were not available for this boat. They needed to measure the entire boat structure and all of its components to create their own drawings and engineering documents. (Author's collection)

Figure 14. *PV-70,* which has been painted *PT-9,* has been lightered back to the Elco Naval Division Plant. The boat has undergone sea trials while in Groton, Connecticut. Here she is being off-loaded from the crane barge. (Author's collection)

Figure 15. *PV-70* has now been designated *PT-9* by Elco and painted in light navy grey and white tones. Her original Rolls Royce Merlin engines have been replaced by the supercharged Packard marine engines. In this photo taken in June 1940, the boat carries the famed Mosquito Fleet emblem on her forward superstructure. This time trial occurred in Groton, Connecticut. (Author's collection)

Figure 16. Another look at *PT-9* in Groton, Connecticut. This sleek 70-foot design was the prototype for Elco's first ten boats. None would see service with the US Navy as an operating squadron during war time; instead, they were given to the British in a Lend-Lease program. (Author's collection)

Figure 17. In this sequence of photos taken on November 4, 1940 this first shot shows Elco's first production run of *PT-10*. Here she is being backed out of the huge sliding doors in front of building 21. Notice the two small tugs being used to pull her and the cradle on wheels (Author's collection)

Figure 18. This nice stern shot of the boat shows her three propellers. Notice the six exhaust ports on the stern. They are straight piped at this time and offer no mufflers, which were adopted on later models to make the boats very quiet. Exhaust gas on later models will be pushed out below the water line (Author's collection)

Figure 19. The boat is now hooked into the dockside crane. Here she will be gently lifted out over the concrete roadway and into the basin. When lowered into the water, the boat will float free of the cradle and be towed to the wet boat basin for other assembly. (Author's collection)

Figure 20. Workers have gathered around the concrete roadway to see Elco's first produced PT boat. Made using blueprints from the British Scott-Paine design, she is gently put into the basin. Her rear cabin trunk has yet to be attached, as other assembly steps will now be taken. This is a historic day for the Elco Naval Division and its workers. (Author's collection)

Figure 21. A busy day at the launching of *PT-10.* On board are members of the NBC radio crew that is doing a live broadcast. In the center (smiling) is U.S. Navy Supervisor of Ship Building, Captain. F.W. Rowe Jr. This event was broadcast to all of New York and New Jersey. (Author's collection)

Figure 22. Many important people were invited to the ceremony celebrating the launching of *PT-10*. Seen here on the bow of *PT-10* are second from left: Henry R. Sutphen, Executive Vice President of Elco, and to his left, the Secretary of the Navy, Charles Edison. Edison would become known as "the father of the PT boat service" for his tireless efforts in pushing to obtain Congressional funding for the program. (Author's collection)

Figure 23. Elco's Managing Constructor, Irwin R. Chase, stands by the forward cabin of *PT-10*. You can clearly see some of the equipment now installed on the boat. Notice the Searchlight, Air horn, and Range Finder (IFF) on the bridge. The large Mosquito (on cabin structure) carrying a Torpedo would become the symbol for the PT boat service. It was designed and delivered by Walt Disney. (Author's collection)

Figure 24. *PT-10* starts to pull away from the outdoor boat shed (under her own power) as workers and engineers stand on deck. By this time many of the workers have gone back to work. A typical day at the Elco Naval Division. (Author's collection)

Figure 25. A nice look at *PT-10* as she runs past the number #2 Channel marker in Newark Bay. Notice the powerful wake produced by the three large Packard marine engines. Elco constantly tried to eliminate this wake throughout the war, but with very little success. Engineers onboard will make notes during Trials clocking the boat's speed, engine performance, and maneuverability. (Author's collection)

Figure 26. The jig or pattern of this seventy foot PT boat has been laid onto the assembly floor. Here a series of numbered frames are being placed onto the jig. When completed, it will form the hull from bow to stern, with all water tight doors installed. This framework will undergo many assembly stages before completed. (Author's collection)

Figure 27. The jig continues to take shape as more of the numbered frames are added. These frames were so light weight that one man could pick them up and place them into the jig. Many changes over the years responded to the need for added strength for areas that were too weak. Yet, when completed, the hull had incredible strength to withstand the constant pounding of the sea. (Author's collection)

Figure 28. The jig with its many frames has been completed and now the keel has been added. Workers have started to assemble batten strips on the boat's bottom and sides. The boat starts to take shape as you watch. (Author's collection)

Figure 29. The hull, with frames attached, is having the wooden batten strips attached to the boat. It is from these strips that the first layer of mahogany planking will be added. There is much work to be completed before the hull can be turned right side up. Notice the stack of wood which will be cut up to make the battens and mahogany planking. (Author's collection)

Figure 30. A look at the joiner shop located in building 21. This upper mezzanine level was ideal for making small parts and other structures. Here a rear cabin trunk structure is being framed for a seventy-foot PT boat. You can clearly see the light weight construction that went into the making of this cabin trunk. When completed, the structure was simply hoisted to the first floor of the assembly area and mounted on the hull. (Author's collection)

Figure 31. Another look at the joiner shop, showing the cabin trunk structures in different stages of assembly. When Elco switched to the seventy-seven foot boats and the final designed eighty-footer, the joiner shop discontinued making cabin structures in this location. There simply was not enough room, and only smaller parts for the boats were completed here. (Author's collection)

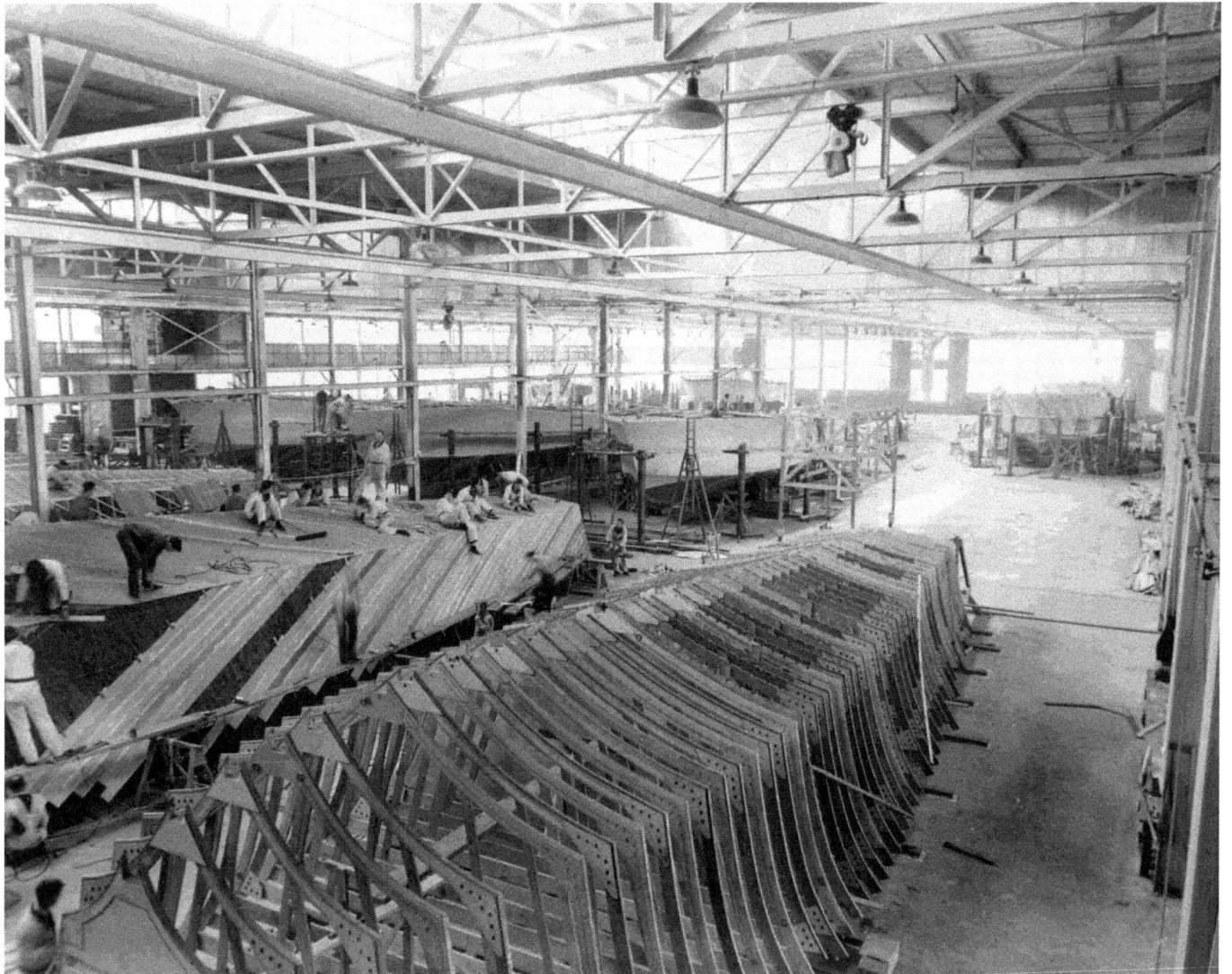

Figure 32. With frames being added to the jig on the right, workers have started to add the mahogany planking to the hull on the left. Workers simply crawled on top of the Hull to complete their work process. This Elco innovation of building the Hull from bottom up certainly made it much easier for workers to perform their work from a less cramped position. (Author's collection)

Figure 33. Workers get set to turn over the massive hull of this boat. Turning straps are in place and the winches and cables ready to go. You can clearly see the beautiful lines of the hull and the quality workmanship that went into the making of the boat. Many types of wood were used in the construction process. Double planked mahogany was one type of wood used. Over this construction, workers would spread airplane cloth on the entire surface, using glue and hot irons to impregnate the wood. (Author's collection)

Figure 34. A noon-time custom at Elco gives workers the chance to operate the controls used to turn over the massive hulls. Construction of the hull in the over turned position was an Elco innovation. It gave workers the room they needed to construct the hull, working on them from above, rather than a cramped position below. Notice the workers riding the hull as it is slowly being turned. They are keeping an eye on the winches and metal cables attached to the turning straps. (PT Boats Inc., Germantown, Tennessee)

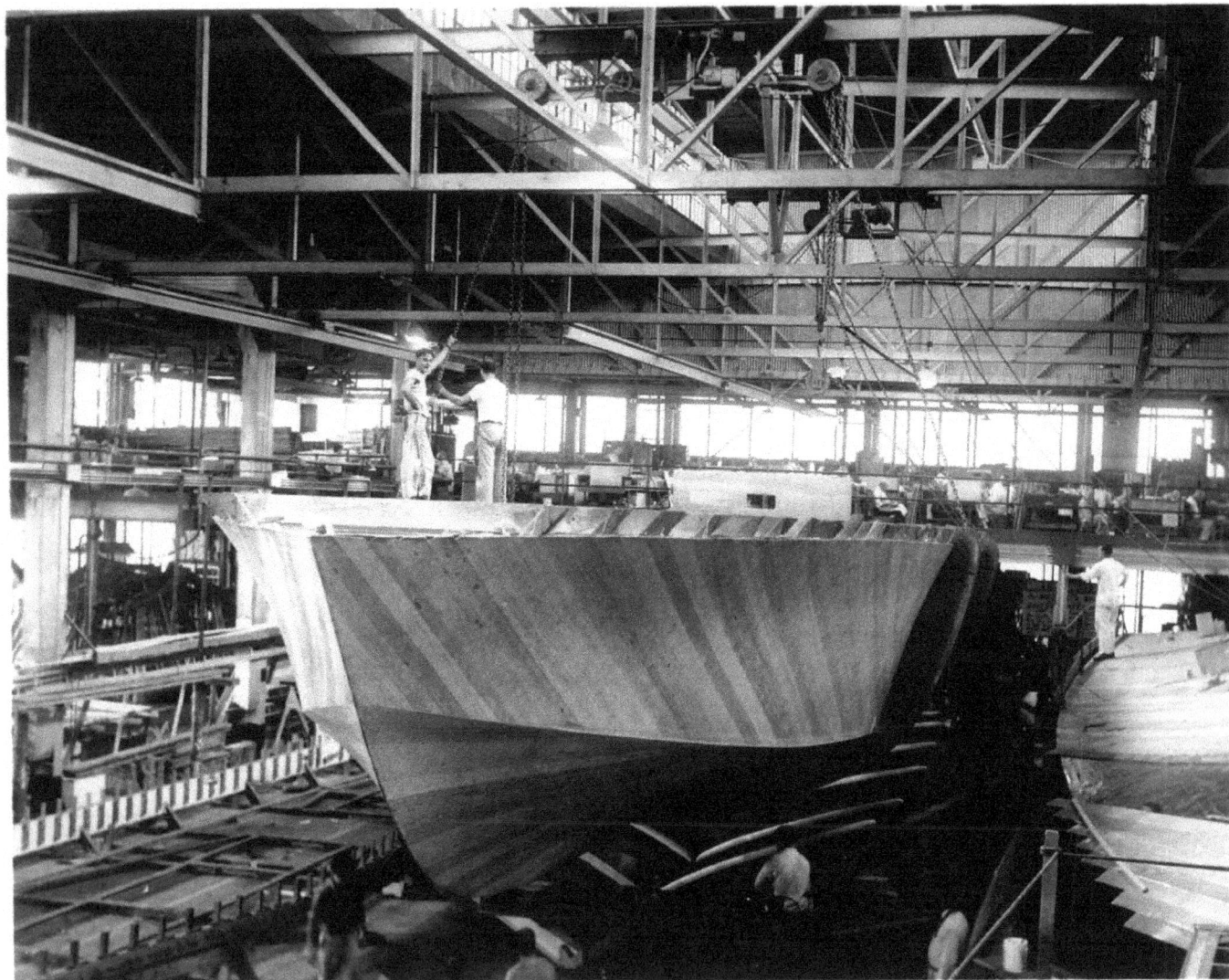

Figure 35. The massive hull of this PT boat has now been completely turned over. From here she will continue through many phases of assembly, eventually making her way thru the large doors and into the waiting dockside carne. The hull sits on a cradle and will be pulled using small tow motors. Notice the wonderful lines of her hull, showing the double planked mahogany used in the construction. The hull now weighs roughly 9 tons. (PT boats Inc, Germantown, Tennessee)

Figure 36. A wonderful look at Elco's 70 Foot PT boat under construction. The hull has been completed and the forward cabin has been put into place. Notice the toe rails which surround the edge of the boat's bow. This photo was taken around August 2, 1940. (Author's collection)

Figure 37. Another look at the building stages for the seventy-foot PT boats. Most of the boats have had their hulls completed and turned right side up. This phase of assembly shows the boats with and without decking, while the boat in the center has its decking in place. The forward cabin has been installed, awaiting workers to continue the process of adding toe rails, hatches, and other equipment. (Author's collection)

Figure 38. A beautiful look at *PT-20* that was Elco's first seventy-seven foot boat. She carried the new 21 inch Mk. VIII torpedo's in the standard issue Mk. XVIII torpedo tubes. At this point, she is still equipped with the PLEXIGLAS® turrets that were removed beginning with *PT-45*. Moisture buildup and fogging over hindered the gunners, thus making it difficult to track any target. *PT-20* would see service with Squadron one, and would be at Pearl Harbor during the Japanese attack. Later she would see service in the Aleutian Islands. (Author's collection)

Figure 39. This hydraulic press was used on the girders that supported the massive engine weight and fuel supply deep in the boat. Two layers of hollowed mahogany plywood between a plywood cover on either side helped to give maximum strength with the least possible weight. It took fourteen hours in this press to complete the process of binding wood with glue under pressure. (PT Boats Inc., Germantown, Tennessee)

Figure 40. Gluing techniques made the wood able to withstand the salt, air and water, making for a great advance in the craft of wooden boat building. Laminated mahogany with a phenolic glue process helped shape the frames that would become the boat's ribs in a standard molded form. Locked together in this form, the frame was taken to this oven and heated to 140 degrees for two hours making wood and glue one. (PT Boats Inc., Germantown, Tennessee)

Figure 41. In building 21, these workers are using screw guns in the fabrication process. It took over 400,000 screws to complete one 80 foot PT boat. (PT Boats Inc., Germantown, Tennessee)

Figure 42. The wooden molded form process is being completed by these two Elco employees. When completed, the wood will have bulldog strength and great endurance. After a time in the oven, this form is removed, than taken out and sanded. (PT Boats Inc., Germantown, Tennessee)

Figure 43. This photo shows the ease and simplicity of this portable Eclipse spray painting equipment. This Elco worker is spraying the PT boat's waterline. Using these sprayers allowed work to progress that much faster. Notice the large steel cradle the boat sits in. (PT Boats Inc., Germantown, Tennessee)

Figure 44. These workers in building 23, the spray shop, are using power sprayers to paint some of the hundreds of parts used in the construction of PT boats. It is said that over a ton of paint was used on each boat. Parts needed to be protected from salt water spray and other elements that the boats would encounter. (PT Boats Inc., Germantown, Tennessee)

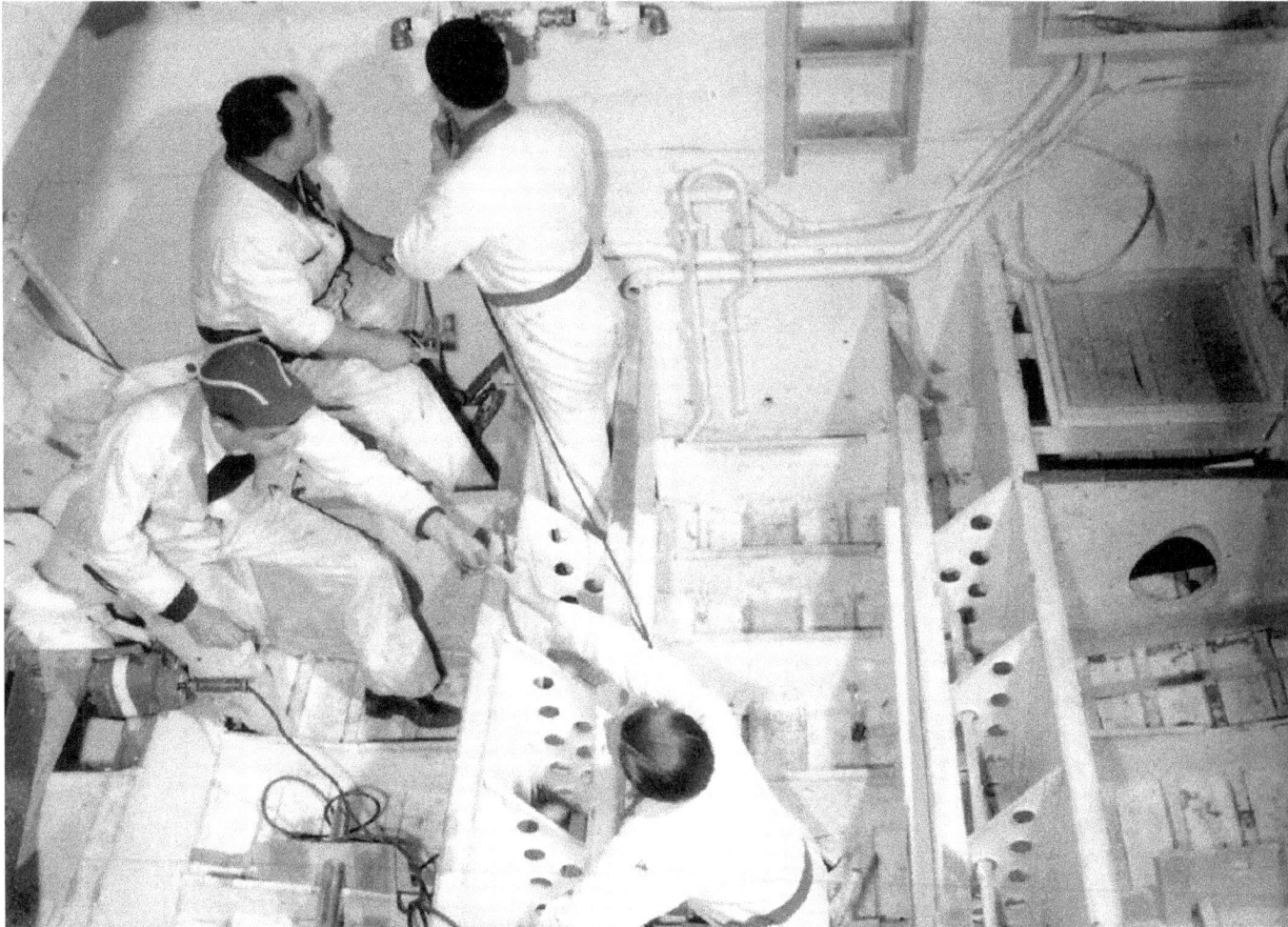

Figure 45. Known as the engine room gang, these workers are busy in the engine room compartment. Two of the workers (rear) are working on plumbing on the aft watertight bulkhead. The worker that is seated is holding a combination square, while the other has an electric drill. Notice the girders and engine beds that will soon carry the three Packard marine engines. (Ed Behney)

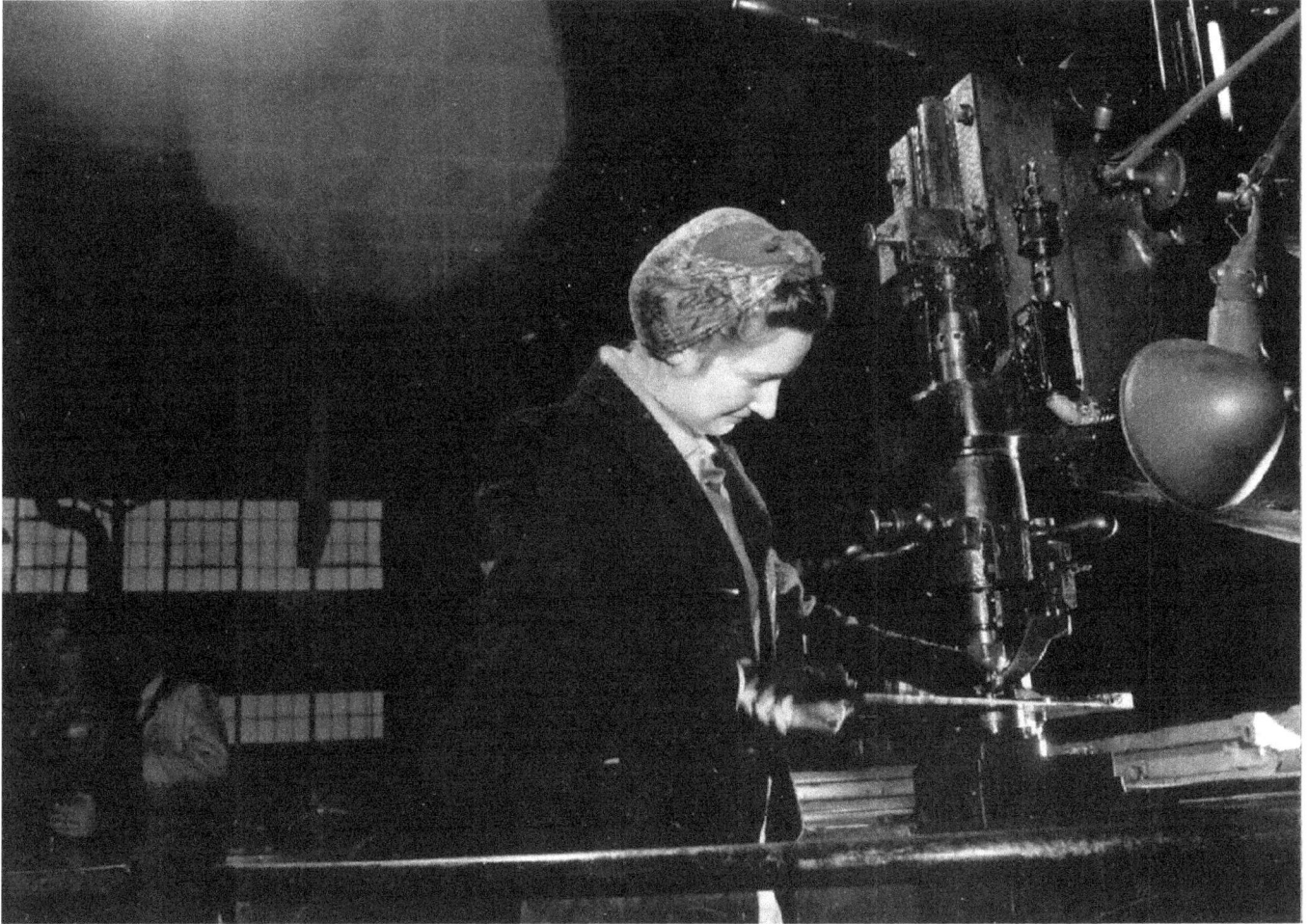

Figure 46. This woman is busy running a machine press in the metal shop. Women were hired at Elco as more men were being drafted into the service. They performed their jobs very well, as Rosie the Riveter was born. (PT Boats Inc., Germantown, Tennessee)

Figure 47. The Elco metal shop produced the many parts needed to complete the boats. In this picture taken in 1943, a female worker is busy operating a brake machine. Notice the overalls and patent leather shoes: typical dress for the women who worked at Elco. (PT Boats Inc., Germantown, Tennessee)

Figure 48. This worker is operating a pneumatic driven grinder, smoothing welded joints on a welded steel support frame. Directly behind him is a very large sheet metal brake, sometimes called a bending brake. Note the sign which reads you will be terminated if using anything thicker than 16 gauge material. PT boats relied on speed and being able to out-maneuver anything afloat. Excess weight was very important. Ounces added up to pounds. (Ed Behney)

Figure 49. This worker in building 21 is cutting smaller wood pieces used in the sub-assembly process. He is using a Walker Radial Machine. Notice the stacks of wood directly under his machine. Taken in June 1944. (PT Boats Inc., Germantown, Tennessee)

Figure 50. March 6, 1944. This Elco employee is using a hand powered drill with a long shaft bit to drill the hole for the eye towing and installation gear. This installation was done on the bow of the boat. The eye towing gear was essential should the boat need to be towed after damage in battle, or upon engine failure. (PT Boats Inc., Germantown, Tennessee)

Figure 51. Women workers stand on scaffolding in building 21, as they work to complete the mahogany planking process. You can clearly see the amount of work it took to complete one PT boat hull. The hull alone, when completed, weighed twelve tons. (PT Boats Inc., Germantown, Tennessee).

Figure 52. Two Elco workers rivet some of the large girders used on the boats. It was not uncommon to complete stages of sub assembly outside of the shop area in good weather as indicated by this photo taken on June 30, 1942. These girders provided maximum stability in all types of weather despite their light weight. (PT Boats Inc., Germantown, Tennessee)

Figure 53. Elco's oldest employee, Frederick Bulkeley (right) who was hired on April 16, 1942. When Bulkeley tried to enlist in the Navy, he was told that he was too old. Newspapers carried this story and shortly after, Bulkeley received over 200 offers for employment. Bulkeley choose Elco because of his past boat building experience. At 76 years of age, Bulkeley went to work each day performing his job, and at times doing promotional work for the Company. His son was the famous Lt. John D. Bulkeley, who gained fame with Squadron 3 in the Philippines. (Author's collection)

Figure 54. Hundreds of parts that were needed in the assembly of the PT boats were shipped in daily from many different outside contractors. Because of the many buildings that were used in the sub-assembly process, Elco built its own railway system no bigger than an amusement park ride. Moving these items on that rail system was this small locomotive nicknamed, "Shifty," as in the eighth little dwarf. (PT boats Inc., Germantown, Tennessee)

Figure 55. This Elco worker is checking one of the large gas tanks to be sure of the proper installation of the rubber coating applied to the tanks before they were placed in the boat. These tanks were pressure checked for any leaks or deficiencies. Each PT was capable of holding 3,000 gallons of high octane fuel in its self sealing tanks. (PT Boats Inc., Germantown, Tennessee)

Figure 56. This photo shows one of several small electric welder stations used by the welding shop. Many women workers were trained as welders by Elco and were reported to have done a superior job during the war years. (PT Boats Inc., Germantown, Tennessee)

Figure 57. June 16, 1942 finds these Elco workers taking advantage of the nice weather as they work outside the shop area riveting structural components to a bulkhead wall. Using a pneumatic rivet hammer they work together making a tight strong fit. (PT Boats Inc., Germantown, Tennessee)

Figure 58. Taken from over-head in building 21 is the machine shop where rough castings were ground, machine polished, threaded and shaped to precision measurements. Metal turret lathes and magnetic chuck surface grinders were just a few of the machines found on the shop floor in this area. (PT Boats Inc., Germantown, Tennessee)

Figure 59. This was one of several Tool Cribs in building 21. The Electric Small Tool Department carried everything from sanders and routers to electrical screwdrivers and skill saws. Workers would check out the tools they needed at the beginning of their shift giving the tool crib staff a metal tag with their Elco employee number stamped on it. In this way tool crib staff knew who took out what tool. Employees would get back their stamped tag at the end of the shift. (PT Boats Inc., Germantown, Tennessee)

Figure 60. Elco was very concerned with the disposal of saw dust and wooden scrap. It took great pains to dispose of this potentially combustible material and had several areas to do so. This Elco worker is disposing of wood in one of the saw dust incinerators. Sawdust was actually collected on over-head conveyors and fed thru disposal pipes to the blowers. (PT Boats Inc., Germantown, Tennessee)

Figure 61. This worker is using a hand cart as he makes his way up the ramp to the incinerator for disposal. Notice the collection of scrap wood that has collected outside the ramp area. Workers on three shifts fed the incinerators on a constant basis to insure a ship-shape factory. (PT Boats Inc., Germantown, Tennessee)

Figure 62. A look at the fabric shop at Elco. Here women workers made many items for the boats including seat cushions and bunk cushions for the crew's quarters. Also made here were seating cushions, dinning table cushions, and bunk cushions for the skipper and his executive officer. (Ed Behney)

Figure 63. War Bond drives and noon-time entertainment were common at Elco. Set up just in front of building 18 (a temporary storage building) these entertainers are busy playing and singing for the workers. Many times Elco workers would provide the entertainment, as seen here at lunch, sometime in 1944. (Author's collection)

Figure 64. This 1942 photo shows the original building which housed the Electro Dynamics Works. This was one of many complexes on the Elco site. Electric motors and generators were constructed here and used by the U.S. Navy for many sea going vessels. This plant provided motors and generators for the PT boats as well. Construction of a new building began in April 1942 and all assembly was moved to the new site. Electro Dynamics Works would remain in Bayonne at the Elco site until a fire on April 4, 1963 destroyed almost all of the buildings, (Author's collection)

Figure 65. A look at the two massive Lumber sheds adjacent to building 21. As many different types of wood were used to construct the boats, these outdoor areas provided much needed space. Indoor storage was also used. Notice the guard shack and fence surrounding this area. (Ed Behney)

Figure 66. Two female workers man the switchboard operator's room at Elco. This 1942 photo shows the old location. Later, more spacious quarters were created in building 21. Hundreds of calls daily went through this location, and two more women were added to the switchboard staff. (Ed Behney)

Figure 67. Always willing to ride the boats, Executive Vice President of Elco, Henry R. Sutphen is dressed out in his winter gear. Cold weather was extremely tough on those who had to test the boats in Newark Bay. Sutphen would do this often to see first hand how the boats were being tested. (Ed Behney)

Figure 68. This worker is busy running a Router on the covering board shelf of the boat. He is notching the top outside edges of the structural haul frames, using a template. Wooden PT boats required much work to insure proper fitting of all parts. (Ed Behney)

Figure 69. This Elco worker is shaving the wooden planking at the sheer line of the boat. He is using a powerful worm drive circular saw while being guided by a small trim board that is temporarily attached to the planking. (Ed Behney)

Figure 70. Checking and stacking the metal propeller shafts. These monel shafts had to be fashioned with extremely accurate and precise measurements to counter the three spinning high-torque props of a PT boat. (Ed Behney)

Figure 71. Auxiliary firemen are working in the crew's quarters of this eighty-foot boat. Using a high powered vacuum, they are careful to remove any sawdust from the bilges. Many inspections took place to insure safety and to see that the boats were thoroughly cleaned. (Ed Behney)

Figure 72. Working under the stern of the boat, a worker is busy fitting out one of the bronze struts on this eighty foot boat. You will also notice one of the propeller shafts as it makes its way to the stern. The high speed pitch props are also added at this stage of assembly. Later, as the boats would become more of a gunboat platform, the props would be changed to compensate for added weight. (Ed Behney)

Figure 73. Just another day at Elco for this worker. He is making his way up a wooden ladder to reach the scaffolding that surrounds the boat. Each worker had his own tool box that kept the tools needed for assembly. Scaffolding was made and supplied by the Bergen Point Iron Works Company of Bayonne, New Jersey. Notice the non slip sneakers worn by this worker. (Ed Behney)

Figure 74. This worker is checking the tapered ends on these propeller shafts. Three of these were needed on each boat. At this stage of assembly, he is installing the keyways on each shaft. Made from monel, these shafts could withstand the destructive properties of salt water. (Ed Behney)

Figure 75. Elco worker is shown with a long-handled iron. This tool was used on the hull to heat the glue used to impregnate the wood. Combined with airplane cloth, this method sealed the hull, making it almost impossible to spring a leak. (Electric Boat Company)

Figure 76. This photo shows Preston L. Sutphen, son of Executive Vice President Henry R. Sutphen. Preston began in sales before becoming a part of upper management during the war. Taking over as director and general manager after the War, Preston competed with other builders in the pleasure boating field. Due to large overhead, labor cost, material procurement and Elco's refusal to use cheaper materials, Elco was forced to close what was once a thriving business, Elco finally locked up its business on New Year's Eve, 1949. (Ed Behney)

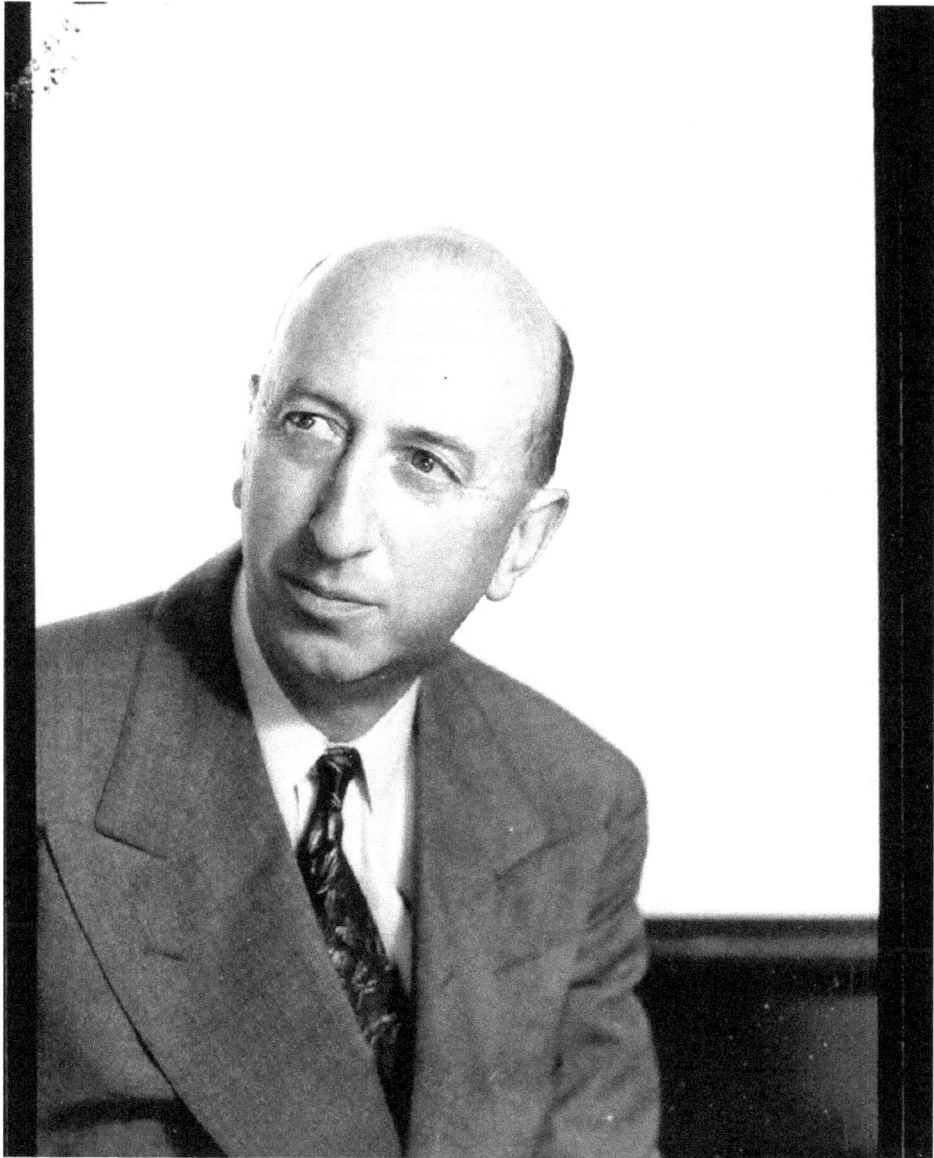

Figure 77. This photo taken in 1943 shows Glenville Sinclair Tremaine. He joined the Elco Company just prior to World War One as Irwin Chase's assistant. In 1923, he became Elco's Chief Naval Architect or Works Manager. Tremaine was a largely self taught designer, who along with Chase and Henry Sutphen, helped build Elco into one of the world's finest builders of cruising pleasure boats. (Ed Behney)

Figure 78. Carrying a heavy (and poorly balanced!) load, this truck is delivering Packard marine engines to the Elco plant. Inside the metal box is the famous 4M-2500 supercharged Engine that powered all of Elco's PT boats. Weighing in at 2,950 pounds, this light weight water cooled engine proved its durability in combat. (Ed Behney)

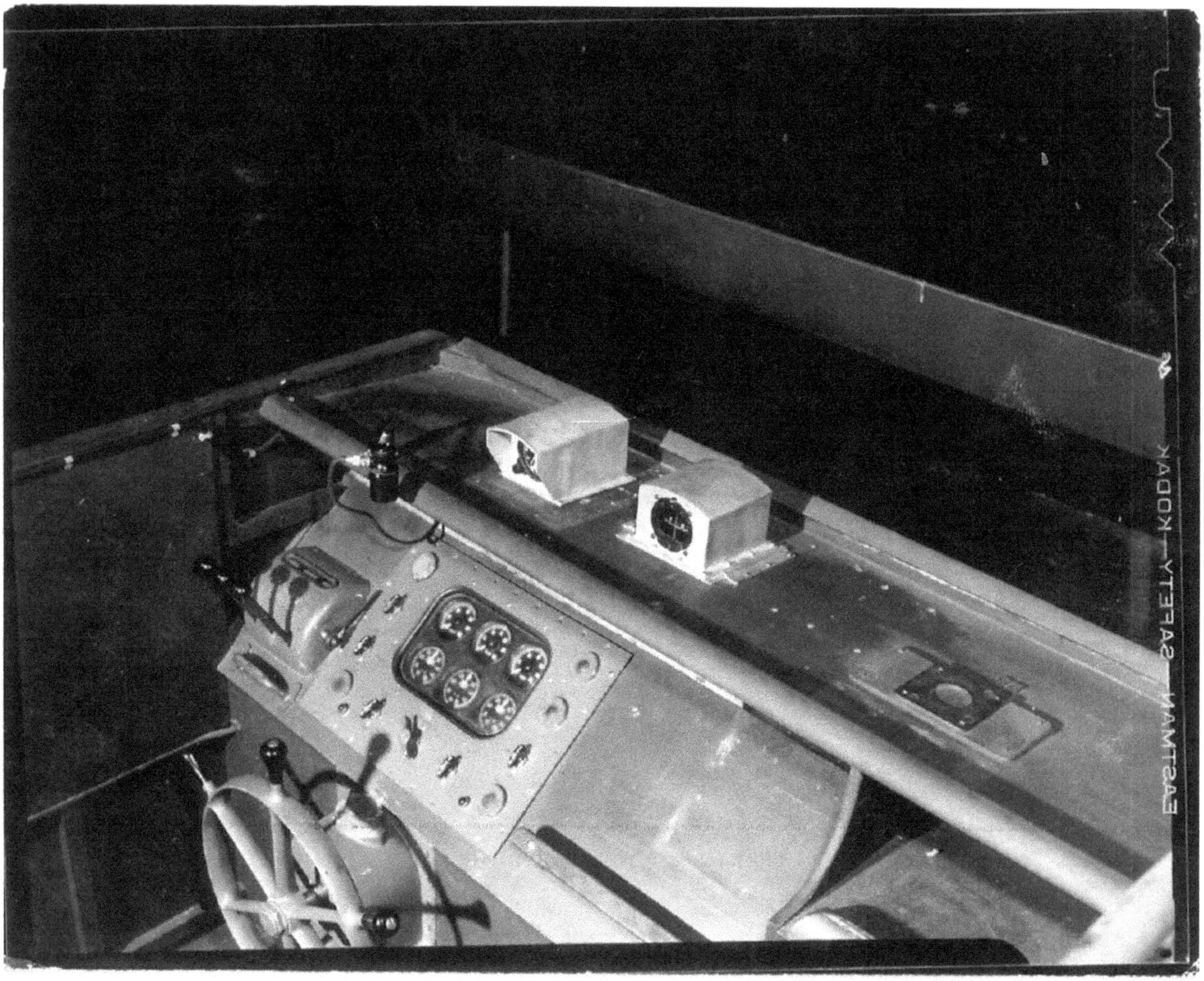

Figure 79. A close up view of the helm of this 80-foot PT boat shows some of the control features. This is an earlier boat set up showing the three throttle controls to the far left of the cockpit. The center panel shows the three tachometer gauges, and the three manifold pressure gauges. Switches around this panel include anchor lights, signal horns, battle switch, engine room buzzer, and emergency lockout switches. The top shelf holds two compasses for navigation. You can also see the boat's wheel. (Ed Behney)

Figure 80. This phase of assembly shows the aft .50-calibre gun tub. Notice the gun suppresser rails built around this tub. This was so a gunner could not shoot into his own boat. Twin .50 calibre Browning machine guns would later be installed in yet another assembly process. (Author's collection)

Figure 81. This phase of assembly involves one of the eighty footer's day room structures. This area provided a space for PT crew members to relax, but could also be used to berth more crew. These structures were made from mahogany plywood giving them durability and lightweight construction. It was because of this surface plywood that many thought the boats were made from this material. When completed, the day rooms were simply hoisted into place and dropped into the deck. Notice one of the forward gun tub assemblies in place on the jig. (Ed Behney)

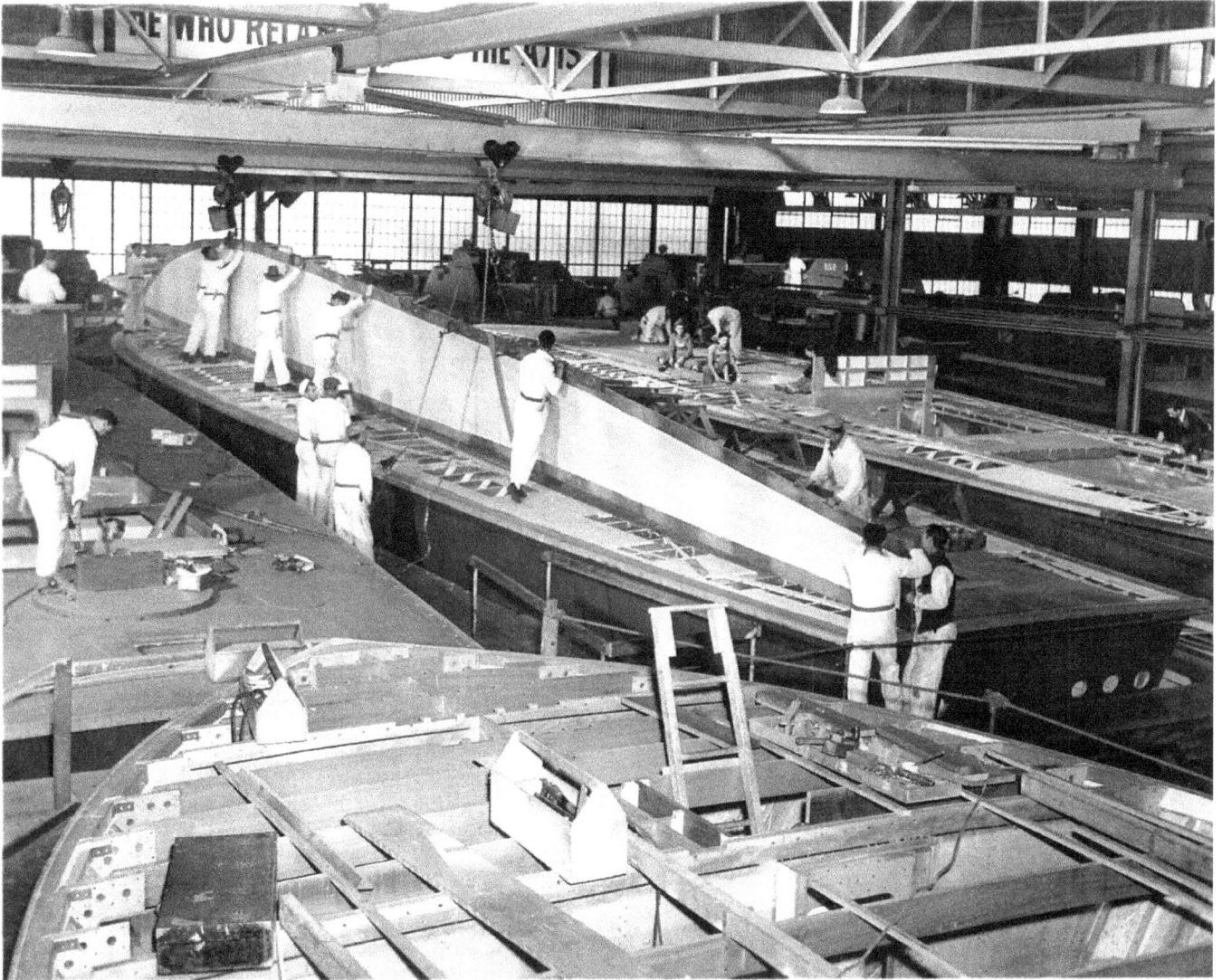

Figure 82. This photo taken in building 21 shows these eighty foot PT boats in different stages of assembly. Workers in the center of the photo have begun to lay down one section of the decking. Elco designers made this as a one piece section, that when put down on the deck it would lie down as flat as a rug. Using two 80-foot sections (all one piece) the top decking would simply be screwed into the framing. (Author's collection)

Figure 83. Building 16 shows these workers installing the center gas tank on this boat. This tank would sit under the day room cabin, one of three gas tanks being Installed. Notice the gas tank is self sealing, which means a bullet passing into the tank would seal itself, thus preventing leaks and possible explosion. In this building, Items such as propellers, rudders, ventilation equipment, wiring, generating equipment, batteries, and fire fighting equipment were installed. It was here that the preparation for placing the boat's armament was made. The boats continued their journey to the wet boat basin for final assembly. (Ed Behney)

Figure 84. A look inside the wet boat basin. These are eighty-foot boats in various stages of assembly. The boats were towed into this enclosure for assembly of weapons systems, ammo boxes, torpedo racks, and other sub-assembly. Notice the large overhead doors, which could be kept closed in the winter, or opened in the summer months. Many windows were made to allow maximum light into the area. These boats would later serve with Squadron 4, based as training boats with the Motor Torpedo Boats Squadrons Training Center at Melville, Rhode Island. (Author's collection)

Figure 85. Another look at the wet boat basin from outside. Notice the large overhead doors. After assembly here, the boats would once again head back to the main assembly plant, and await dockside trials. These trails would include the first engine tests of the powerful Packard marine engines. (Electric Boat Company)

Figure 86. This large barge has the standard XVIII torpedo tubes on board that will be used in the assembly of the boats. These early tubes held the MK VIII torpedo and were fired using a black powder charge. The torpedo was of World War One vintage, and not very reliable. Notice this barge also holds some of the smoke generators as well. (PT Boats Inc., Germantown, Tennessee)

Figure 87. March 16, 1942 is a historic day for the Elco Naval Division. Dockside in front of building 21, *PT-103* gets set to run time trials. This would be Elco's first eighty-foot boat. Navy men and officials are seen on board. On the bridge from the left: Capt. F.W.Rowe, Supervisor of Ship Building; Irwin Chase, Managing Constructor; Capt. George A. Alexander; Henry R. Sutphen, Executive Vice President of Elco; and Capt. G.W. Nelson. Nelson and Alexander were ranking members of the official Navy Trial Board. Also seen in this photo (back row in suit) is Preston Sutphen, General Manager at Elco. Others in the photo are various members of Elco, whose names are unknown. (Electric Boat Company)

Figure 88. Time trials are being held in Newark Bay as *PT-103* makes run number 25. She carries two MK VIII Torpedoes (in black-powder charged tubes) and eight depth charges. Because of its raised freeboard, it was a much larger boat than other Elco designs. Built at a cost of $150,000 the boat displaced 51 tons, with a top speed of 43 knots. During the war, Elco would produce 327 of these boats. *PT-103* would later serve with Squadron 5. (John C. Kenney)

Figure 89. *PT-175* is ready for fuel at the Gulf Marine gas dock. Fueling these boats was tricky business as 100-octane gas was used to feed the throbbing Packard marine engines. Each boat was capable of holding 3,000 gallons of gas in three separate tanks. *PT-175* was placed in service on January 20, 1943, serving with Squadron 11. (PT Boats Inc., Germantown, Tennessee)

Figure 90. A look at the outdoor boat shed to the left of building 21. Boats would be placed here for other assembly procedures and to keep them under cover from prying eyes. Workers are aligning the forward 20mm cannon for limit stops. Notice the fake SO radar dome on top of an early style mast. The boat also carries air flask torpedo tubes. Up to ten boats could be placed in the outdoor boat shed keeping workers out of the elements while working on the boats. (Ed Behney)

Figure 91. This was part of Elco's Fourth of July Entertainment program in 1944. Shown at the helm of this PT boat is Helen Jepson, a well known soprano. She spent much of her career at New York City's Metropolitan Opera. She gained a wider audience with her one attempt at film, *The Goldwyn Follies* (1938), a lavish musical flop. To her left is Irwin R. Chase, Managing Constructor at Elco, showing her how this wonderful boat handles. (Andrew Shannahan)

Figure 92. Awarding of the Fourth Star of the Army-Navy "E" Flag to the Elco Naval Division of the Electric Boat Company, and the World Premiere of Warner Brothers Technicolor film "Devil Boats". This ceremony and showing was held on August 22, 1944, in the Dewitt Theatre, Bayonne, New Jersey. Over 2,800 Elco employees and friends were in the audience that night. To the left of the theatre, the American Legion Band of Richmond County provided a concert as quests arrived. The movie "Devil Boats" was about one man's look into the exciting building, training, and operating an Elco boat in combat. The Theatre first opened on December 20, 1923 and was named in honor of Dewitt Van Buskirk, a prominent Bayonne citizen. (Andrew Shannahan)

Figure 93. These two Elco security guards get set to raise the Army/Navy E Flag above the plant. Presented to the Elco Naval Division, this award was given for Outstanding War Production and excellence in quality and quantity. The U.S. Navy command which had the largest interest in a war production facility (in this case Elco) could nominate that Plant for this award. The five small stars showing on this flag represent Elco receiving this award, a total of five times. (Andrew Shannahan)

Figure 94. In a ceremony at the Elco plant, Henry R. Sutphen (right), Executive Vice President of Elco, presents PT boat hero and Medal of Honor winner, Lt. John D. Bulkeley, a wonderful model of his famed *PT-41*. Bulkeley rescued General Douglas Macarthur from the Philippines as the Japanese were set to take the Island. Bulkeley was flown home where he was instrumental in obtaining recruits for the PT boat service. Bulkeley was also high on the list as part of the War Bond drives and guest speaker duties, often drawing large crowds, and bringing in much money for the War Bond efforts. This model boat was hand built by Fred Rosencrantz, who worked in the hull department at Elco. He built many Factory models and presentation pieces during his employment with Elco. (Electric Boat Company)

Figure 95. April 25, 1942: members of the Navy visit the Elco Plant. During the war, many visitors toured the plant, including Navy brass, well known Senators, Congressmen, PT boat crewmen, and other famous people. They were shown first hand the many different buildings that made up the plant, and the overall assembly of the boats. In this group we see, (second from the left) Robert Montgomery, who would go on to star in many major films, including *They Were Expendable;* Capt. F.W.Rowe; Supervisor of Ship Building; Irwin R. Chase, Managing Constructor at Elco; and Preston Sutphen, General manager at Elco. (Electric Boat Company)

Figure 96. Irwin Chase Sr. (left) is dressed for the elements as he watches his son, Irwin Chase Jr., man the helm of this eighty-foot PT boat. Heading out into Newark Bay, Chase put the boat thru its paces, much to his father's delight. After the tour, Chase Sr. said that his son has all the right stuff to become a fine PT boat skipper. Chase Jr became a decorated veteran when in 1944 he became a Navigator on the fast aircraft carrier *Ticonderoga*. On January 21, 1945, the carrier was attacked by Japanese *Kamikaze* planes near Formosa. With both the Captain and Executive Officer injured, then Commander Chase led successful fire fighting and damage control efforts, bringing the carrier back to its base in Ulithi. Chase was awarded the Silver Star for his actions. He retired in 1959 with the rank of Rear Admiral. (Electric Boat Company)

Figure 97. *PT-39,* a seventy-seven-footer, served with Squadron 3(2) in the defense of Guadalcanal. The boat was shipped back to the Motor Torpedo Boat Squadrons Training Center at Melville, Rhode Island, for training purposes. Seen here on the concrete roadway at Elco, she was sent here for clean up of the hull, and some much-needed painting. The boat was later shipped to New York City for the 6th War Bond Drive. People could get a close up view at this little giant killer. The 6th War Bond drive would raise much needed funds for the war effort. (PT Boats Inc., Germantown, Tennessee)

Figure 98. Elco's invention of working on their hulls from above rather then a cramped position below, led to a noon time custom in building 21. As the hulls were completed, they needed to be turned right side up so that decking and other installations could continue. Workers and even whole departments were chosen to run the controls that turned the massive hulls. It became a custom at Elco throughout the War. Here, Miss McLaughlin and the Welding Foremen and Welders get set to turn the hull of this boat on October 27, 1942. (PT Boats Inc., Germantown, Tennessee)

Figure 99. Here women workers from the Electrical Assembly Department take their place in front of this boat as they get set to turn the massive hull. Signs attached to the hulls were often an incentive to produce more PT boats. This sign reads "Although we are short on the above items, don't let us sell America short on PTs, a PT equals the workmanship and effort you men and women put into it. LET'S GIVE OUR NAVY OUR ALL." (PT Boats Inc., Germantown, Tennessee)

Figure 100. Another eighty-foot PT boat is lowered into the basin by the massive twin boomed Crane. The crane operator must use precision in lowering the boat. When it reaches a certain depth, the boat will float free from the cradle. This was a set up shot using red, white, and blue bunting, and dummy torpedo tubes. It is uncertain as to which numbered boat this is. (Author's collection)

Figure 101. Elco completed an outdoor ball field on the back side of building 21. Here Elco employees could play baseball, softball, football, and soccer. This photo shows the worker's soccer team in the bleachers at one of the local ball fields in Bayonne. (Ed Behney)

Figure 102. Taken in June of 1945, Hull Supervisor John Guttridge takes a big swing during A baseball game behind building 20. Known as the Beltics, employees enjoyed a change from the everyday routine of assembly work. Elco employees would also have their own men and women bowling teams. (Ed Behney)

Figure 103. A late War eighty-foot Elco *(PT-731)* is hoisted out over the concrete roadway in front of Building 21. Notice the Higgins-type pneumatic launching torpedo tubes that have been installed. *PT-731* was one of many American built boats sent to the Soviet Union on the Lend-Lease program during WWII. Prior to transfer of the Elco boats to the USSR, most of the American-built boats were either Higgins seventy-eight footers, or the seventy-foot Vosper's. All Higgins boats had the pneumatic launching torpedo tubes installed. This might explain the installation of the tubes onto Elco boats for Fleet-wide parts and service compatibility reasons. The Higgins tubes also operated better in cold climates. This was the first boat of the Elco series numbered *PT-731* through *790* that was scheduled to be sent to the USSR. *PT-731* was shipped completed, while *PT-732* through *760* were shipped in knocked down kit form. *PTs 761 through 790* were cancelled prior to completion due to the end of the war. (Author's collection)

Figure 104. Taken on October 24, 1945, this photo shows *PT-622* awaiting time trials in Newark Bay. Sitting along side the concrete roadway, some Elco employees and Navy brass turn out for this all important day. This is Elco's last built boat, excepted by the US Navy. She will be placed in Squadron 42, (the last squadron to be formed) slated for the South Pacific. The boat will never make it there, as this Squadron was never shipped to the war zone. (Ed Behney)

HIGGINS INDUSTRIES

Andrew Jackson Higgins owned a small fleet of schooners and brigantines, used for his lumber business. He set up a repair yard for his boats in the Industrial Canal of New Orleans. During the Depression, the lumber supplies in the South were quickly running out, and freight rates dropped quickly. Higgins turned his attention to small boat design and formed Higgins Lumber and Export Company, whose primary purpose was the building of small motorboats. He began experimenting with small watercraft, airboats, and flying boats. During a major flood in 1927 his shallow draft boats were used to save tractors and farm equipment by transporting them up and down the Mississippi and Ohio Rivers. In 1928 Higgins was awarded a contract by a Dutch company to build 20 boats..

The Army Corps of Engineers also wanted several of the boats, which needed to be delivered up the Arkansas River. With the river very high, the water was filled with floating debris. Objects rammed into the bows of the boats, and it was quickly realized that a new bow design would be needed. This bow must ride over over the logs and submerged objects, so Higgins built a 16-foot boat powered by an Evinrude motor. This boat set a record in 1930 by making the journey from New Orleans to St. Louis in 72 hours. Higgins Industries was incorporated in that same year, located in New Orleans. Its main purpose was to fill the needs of local trappers, oilmen and lumbermen. Pleasure boats were also being built, but very few could afford them during the Depression. Higgins boats were known for their speed, durability, and maneuverability. Higgins called his best model the *Eureka* and it could jump floating logs, and turn in its own length at full speed.

By 1937, the US Coast Guard and the Army Corps of Engineers were purchasing Higgins boats, but the US Navy was not interested. Higgins made trips to Washington to try and sell his boats, but he was competing against the large Northeastern yards and the Navy's own Bureau of Construction and Repair (BCR). The BCR were designing their own landing craft and were not interested in what a small-time boat builder from the

South might have developed. After four years of rejections, Higgins was finally awarded a contract by Lt. Commander R.S. McDowell, who was responsible for Landing Craft development in the BRC, and informed that $5,200.00 was available to purchase an experimental 30 foot landing boat. Thus in May of 1939, Higgins was officially awarded a contract from the US Navy. Shortly after, the US Navy became officially interested in the development of fast shallow draft Torpedo Boats.

The Navy was interested in two boats, one a small boat around 54 feet in length, the other around 70 feet. The idea for the first was to field a craft capable of being hoisted on board fleet auxiliaries and cargo vessels. The idea for the second was for a craft suitable for offshore operations. The specs for the second boat called for her to be between 70 and 80 feet overall; capable of being operated by two officers and eight men; have a trial speed of 40 knots, with a minimum cruising radius of 275 miles at top speed and 550 miles at cruising speed. The Navy wanted the boats to be constructed of wood or metal, round-or V hulled; powered by gasoline or diesel; and equipped with at least two .50 caliber machine guns, two 21 inch torpedo tubes, and four depth charges.

Higgins Industries jumped at the chance to become a part of this, and managed to get an invitation to bid. Andrew Jackson Higgins put up his own money and designed *PTs* 5 and 6. These two boats, the first actually contracted (on 25 May 1939), were based on the larger Sparkman and Stephens design, scaled up to 81 feet. Higgins found the submitted design so poor that it developed its own, delivering it to the Navy in February 1941. Higgins also built a 76' craft, one that its naval proponents thought to be superior to the Elco design. This contract signaled the beginning of Higgins Industries' prominent association with the Navy under the dynamic leadership of Andrew Jackson Higgins.

After more testing, the Navy Department decided on three designs with one of them being the Higgins PT boat. The Navy asked Higgins for modifications, primarily an increase in size to improve the overall sturdiness and seaworthiness of the craft. The Navy asked for the boats to be no less than 75 feet long and not more than 82 feet long. The Higgins boats had three Packard marine engines, equipped with mufflers to permit silent approaches.

Trial speed was set at 40 knots, sustainable for one hour; with a cruising radius of 500 miles. As a result of these specifications, Higgins was contracted to build 24 boats, scaled up to 78 feet. Higgins Industries had already outgrown its small St. Charles Avenue plant, and began expansion into a new, larger plant on City Park Avenue. This was the old Albert Weiblen Marble and Granite Works Company. This transformation into a boat building facility would cost a staggering 1.5 million dollars. It had the distinction of being the largest boat manufacturing plant housed under one roof. It was also the first boat building plant to use mass-production techniques to build landing craft.

PT boats completed at City Park were loaded onto flatcars and transported to Bayou St. John for launching and testing in Lake Ponchartrain. During the War years some eight plants in New Orleans produced some 20,000 boats and landing craft for the Allies during WWII. Higgins also pioneered the compressed-air method of firing torpedoes. This was a major advance over the Elco produced black powder charged tubes, as no flash could be detected while firing.

Higgins produced some 199 PT boats during the war, with most of them ending up in the Mediterranean theater. The first class of Higgins PT boats was the *PT-71* class. This 78-footer did not have the graceful lines of the 80' Elco boats, but had a much tighter turning radius. This was an important feature when the boats were used in the role of barge busting, or when they needed to evade enemy planes. This boat displaced some 43 tons and could achieve a top speed of about 40 knots. Above decks the Higgins had a spacious deck, although the chart house was a bit small and more forward to the bow.

The cockpit, which was just aft of the charthouse, was situated between the two plywood turrets that held the twin .50 calibre Browning machine guns. This set up gave the gunners a limited field of fire. Half the length of the hull was taken up by the engine room compartment, making for a large and spacious engine room, but a small and cramped crew's quarters. The mufflers were located at the sides of the boats, and the boats carried two 700-gallon gasoline tanks in the engine room.

Originally, these boats carried the Mk-VIII Torpedoes, but this was later changed to the Mk-XIII in roll off racks. The early boats in this class carried the 20mm cannon on the stern, but over the years different weapons were added to combat enemy surface craft. Higgins received the Army-Navy E Flag several times during the War (the highest award bestowed upon a civilian company) for excellence in design and productivity. The contribution of Andrew Jackson Higgins, his business, and his employees to the war effort was so great, that even Adolf Hitler was aware of Higgins, referring to him as "the new Noah."

Higgins Industries stayed in business after the war, building pleasure craft, including the 17 foot Delux Utility pleasure boat, its 19 foot Delux runabout, cabin cruisers, and unique amphibious camp trailers. As with Elco, Higgins had its share of problems, including a walk-out by workers for more money, the U.S. Government's decision to sell thousands of army and navy surplus boats to the public, and a hurricane causing more than $3 million in damages. The hurricane hit New Orleans on September 19, 1947, with the center of this massive storm passing over the city at 9:30 am.

The hurricane threw completed boats into one another, ruined plant machinery, and covered the plant with debris, mud, and logs. The place was a mess, which took the last of Higgins's money. He put all his remaining capital into producing pleasure boats and camp trailers and in finding the materials, labor and new production lines for wooden toilet seats and oak block flooring. Because the damage was caused by flooding, the insurance company did not cover the loss.

To add to these problems, Higgins's son Frank talked his father into buying a substitute wood for use in making marine plywood. Used in making hundreds of pleasure craft, this inferior wood began rotting from the inside out. At his own expense, Higgins brought these boats back to the plant and had them redone, a massive undertaking which consumed much-needed cash. By the fall of 1948, Higgins, Inc.'s future looked bleak. The company was out of money and the large pool of consumer money that was available when the "E" bonds were cashed in at the end of the war had dried up.

Not to be defeated, Higgins built his business back up, thanks in part to the Korean War. On November 9, 1951, Higgins got a contract to build ten 165 foot wooden minesweepers, not to mention securing a contract to build fourteen 65' cargo and pleasure vessels. Another 32 boats were later added to this contract. This increased his government contracts to $30 million dollars.

Unfortunately, Higgins died on August 1, 1952, at the age of sixty-five. At the time of his death, his company had commercial and military contracts totaling more then $61 million dollars. Higgins Industries stayed busy; the last of its minesweepers were completed in 1955. Higgins continued doing repair work and building new commercial craft, oil field platforms, supply boats, and pleasure craft. The company expanded the north side of the shipyard, but the yard was becoming much too large to compete against the smaller yards, yet too small to bid against larger companies.

The yard was greatly affected by the steel strike of 1957. It gambled and purchased $2 million worth of metal to be prepared in case of another strike. Higgins now had the steel but no contracts. By 1959, Higgins was again in financial trouble, and ultimately sold out to New York Ship to pay outstanding debts. Presently, Trinity Marine operates the Industrial Canal plant. Today where the St. Charles Avenue plant once stood is a restaurant. Where the City Park plant was located is the New Orleans Municipal Training Center for police and firemen, and an extension of Delgado College.

Figure 105. Andrew Jackson Higgins at his City Park plant. He rose to international prominence during World War II for his design and mass production of naval combat motorboats—boats that forever changed the strategy of modern warfare. He was larger than life, a small southern businessman who would become head of one of the largest industrial complexes in the United States. (Culver Pictures Inc.)

Figure 106. A look at the City Park plant. With construction beginning in July 1940, it cost some $1.5 milllion dollars to transform the Albert Weiblen Marble and Granite Works into a boat building facility. This new shipyard became one of the world's largest boat manufacturing plants housed under one roof. PT boats built here were shipped by flat car, using the Southern Railway system, to Bayou St. John. There the boats were launched and tested in Lake Pontchartrain. (Navy Archives)

Figure 107. These three Higgins workers are busy on this PT boat. Here they are using clamped jigs for alignment, notching, and installation of a major longitudinal beam near the chine to frames in the starboard bow. This appears to be in the forward crew's quarters of the boat. (Navy Archives)

Figure 108. Workers are installing anchor blocks between the frames for attaching the first course of inner diagonal planking to the keel. The anchor blocks provide an attachment point and transition between the keel and the diagonal planking. These workers are very near the bow of the boat, approximately at frames 5-10. Notice how the prefabricated frames are constructed using solid beams covered with laminated mahogany and bolts. The oval shaped holes are for bilge draining. (Navy Archives)

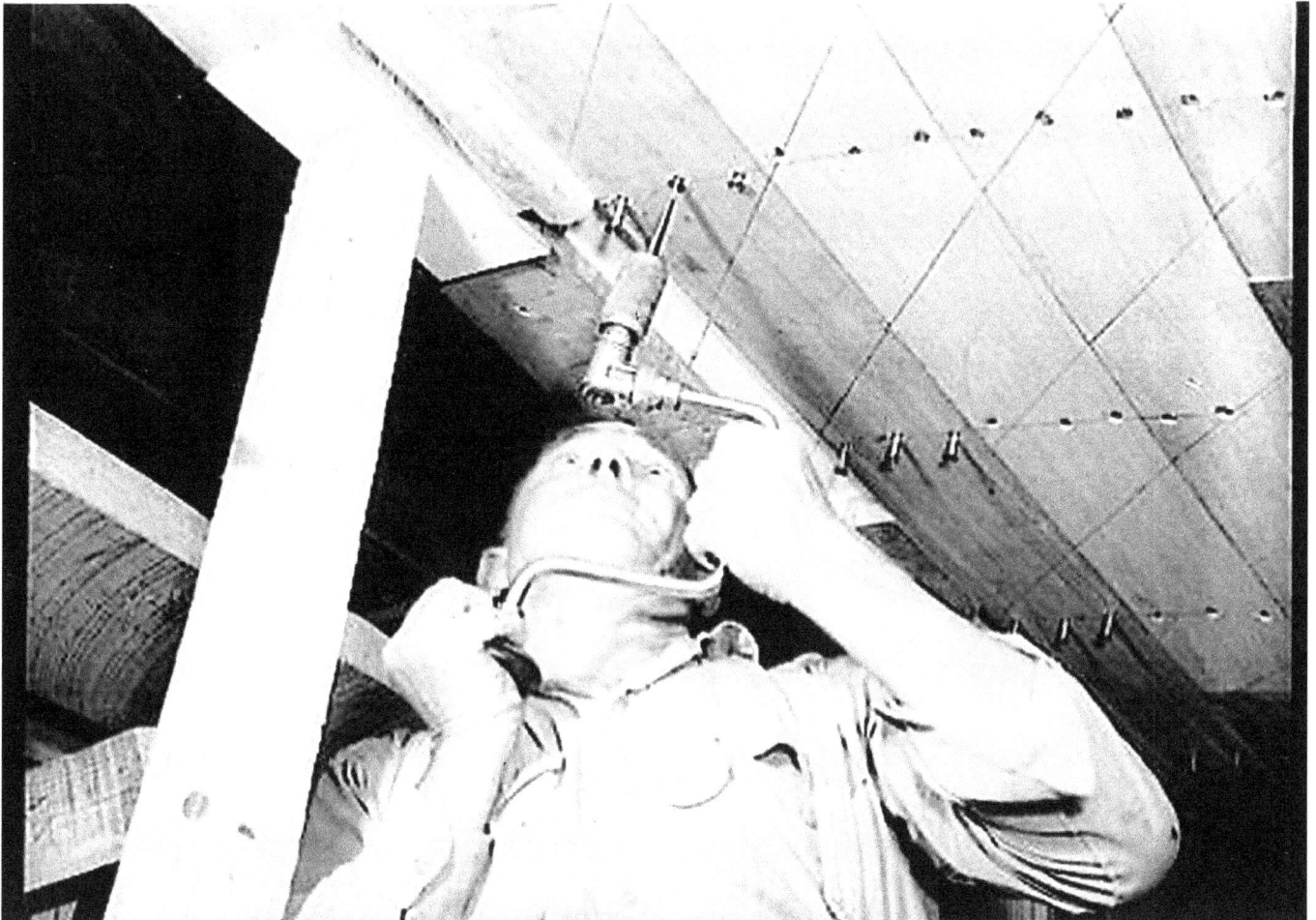

Figure 109. This craftsman is starting to attach the outer layer of ¾' thick mahogany bottom planking via predrilled holes, through inner diagonal planks and into transverse frames on bottom of the stern near chine. This is aft starboard just outboard of propeller using 2' bronze screws with a brace and bit. The holes will later be plugged with wooden bungs. (Navy Archives)

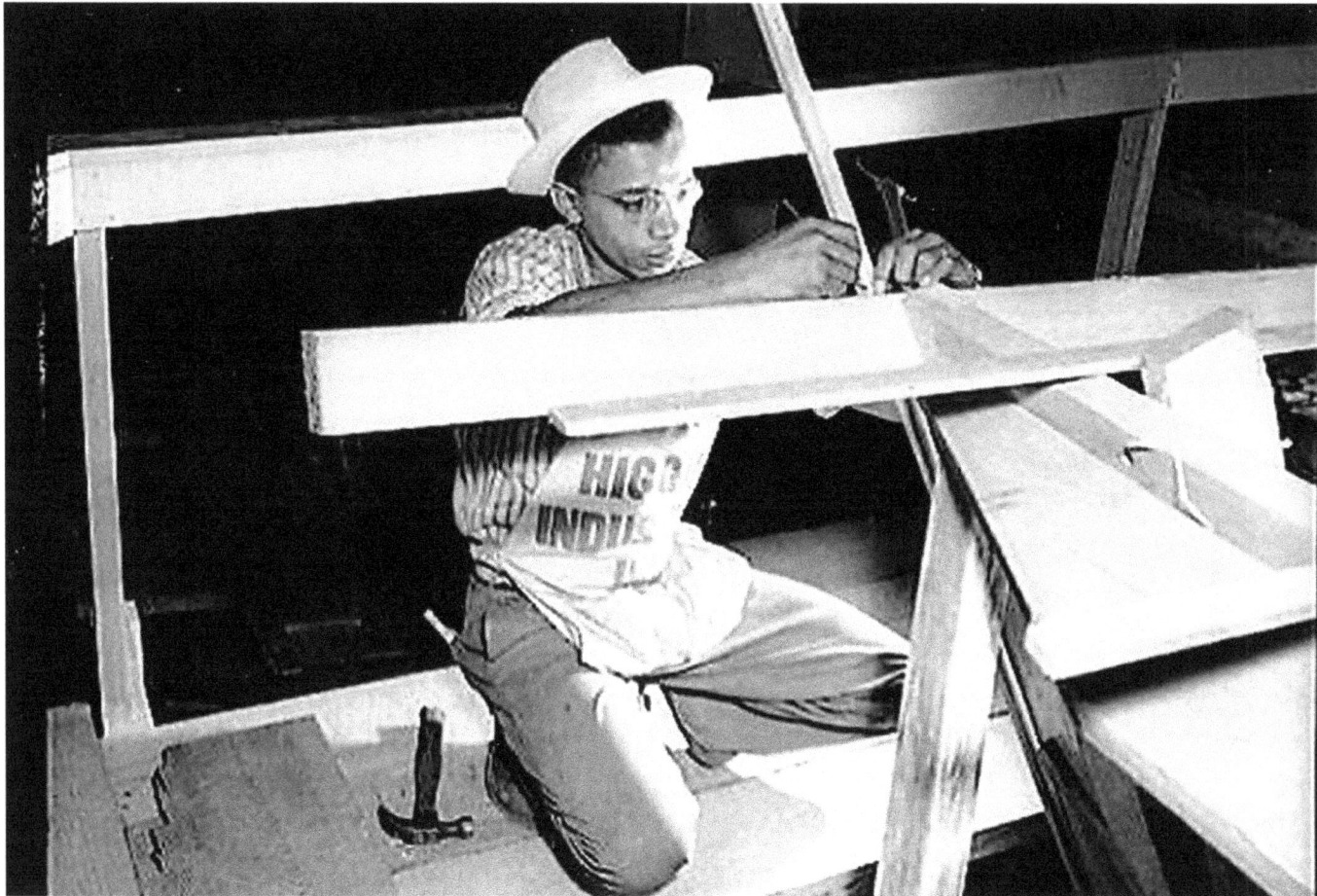

Figure 110. Here is an interesting aspect of Higgins Industries. They hired black workers during the war to work on the boats, even though segregation in the military was in effect at this time in history. Higgins had one assembly line for blacks only and even established a separate trade school to train black laborers. This worker is taking measurements to insure all parts fit like a glove. (Navy Archives)

Figure 111. This is one of several massive lumber buildings that Higgins had. Notice the many prefab sections in stock. As with other companies that built PT boats, the amount of lumber on hand was staggering. Higgins Industries used more than the others as they were also building wooden landing craft and other small boats. Higgins built some twenty-thousand different water craft during the war. (Navy Archives)

Figure 112. Higgins secured specifications from the Navy and built *PT-5* and *PT-6*. This eighty-one-footer was a Sparkman and Stevens design. Here, the first *PT-6* has been loaded onto a mobile cradle and is being pulled through the streets of New Orleans. Once at the Bayou St. John, the boat will be offloaded, launched and tested. (Navy Archives)

Photograph No. 107.

Show boat as originally launched.
Chine rail originally placed was
removed and replaced with heavier
rail shown on previous photographs.

Figure 113. *PT-6* has been launched in the Bayou St. John and is awaiting further tests. Higgins suggested changes to this design, but the Navy Department was very resistant to his recommendations. In April 1940, this Sparkman and Stevens design, approved by the Navy and built by Higgins, could not pass the U.S. military's acceptance trials. Realizing that *PT-6* was unstable in its present state, Higgins virtually rebuilt the boat, agreeing to sell it to the Finnish government. The boat would later be sold to the United Kingdom in June 1940. (Navy Archives)

Figure 114. *PT-6* along with *MRB-2* is tied up along the dock. *MRB-2* was a seventy-six foot design, using 900-hp Hall Scott engines and tried out by Higgins. *PT-6* was later designated MGB 68 while with the British Navy. (Navy Archives)

Figure 115. A nice look at *PT-5* and *PT-6* tied up at the Higgins Marina and gas docks located on the Bayou St. John. Boats heading out to Lake Pontchartrain could gas up here, along with other small boat repairs. This was also a showroom for the Higgins small pleasure boats. (Navy Archives)

Photograph No. 1.
Note heavy type of rails at bow
and chine. Contribute to having
a "dry boat".

Figure 116. Higgins's second design numbered *PT-6* was called Prime, which he built to his own specifications. The Navy once again stepped in, with inspectors forcing him to make changes to the hull and add weight in outfitting the craft. This new design would prove superior to both the earlier *PT-5* and the first *PT-6*. Here the boat is running builder's trials. (Navy Archives)

Figure 117. Another look at *PT-6* Prime as she runs builder's testing. Although not having torpedoes or guns, the boat carries extra weight (pig iron) to simulate the extra weight that will be added later. This extra weight was simply placed on the deck by the Navy, resulting in damage to the hull. The boat later ran tests for the Navy called "the Plywood Derbies" with the boat running an average speed of 31.40 knots over the 190-mile course. Although not the fastest, this Higgins design would have a smaller turning radius then the Elco boat, with the Huckins design rated the best. (Navy Archives)

Figure 118. The man himself, Andrew Jackson Higgins, rides his design during some of the builder's testing on Lake Ponchartrain. The engine room hatch is open with engineers at the ready. This boat used three supercharged Vimalert gasoline engines, putting out 4,050 hp. The boat would prove far superior to both *PT-5* and *PT-6 (1)*. (Navy Archives)

Photograph No. 17.
Radio compartment on port
side of boat from galley.

Figure 119. A look at the somewhat comfortable radio room compartment on the port side, complete with cushioned chair, table, and cabinets. (Navy Archives)

Figure 120. A hearty meal could be cooked on *PT-6 Prime* in this very spacious galley. Notice the many drawers and cabinets. A nice sink with running water and a two burner stove rounded out the area. Higgins spared no expense as you look at what seems to be a full sized refrigerator. (Navy Archives)

Figure 121. A very well put together Officer's Room with all the comforts. To the left is the enclosed head, a desk with fold out lid and cabinet space, and to the right a closet for hanging clothes. (Navy Archives)

Photograph No. 19,

Officers' ward room.
No, this is not a hotel room.

Figure 122. Another look at the Officers Room with comfortable bunk space, complete with drawers and to the left a drop down table (Navy Archives)

Figure 123. A look at the crew's quarters in *PT-6 Prime* looking aft. Notice the ladder to the pilot house. This area was actually roomy with comfortable bunks and a good amount of headroom. (Navy Archives)

Figure 124. A great look at the enclosed pilot house of *PT-6 Prime*. All controls and levers are within easy reach of the operator. The hatch to the center was a companion way to the crew quarters. This design was completely changed in the new *PT-71* class boat. (Navy Archives)

1.

78 PT 71 - 94
197 -254
PORT QUARTER VIEW
PT 74
CONTRACT NO. 94729 AND 94729 OPTION 1
HIGGINS INDUSTRIES INC.
NEW ORLEANS LA. U.S.A.
8-5-42

Figure 125. From the results of Navy testing, it was decided that the boats should be more durable, easier to maneuver, and designed for properly firing guns and torpedoes. Higgins changed the design completely, opting to build a boat that wasn't so beamy and was stronger, steeper, and heavier than *PT-6 Prime*. This new design began with his *PT-71* class boat. At seventy-eight feet, the boat could attain a top speed of forty-one knots. Here we see *PT-74* being constructed at the Higgins Industries City Park plant in New Orleans. (Navy Archives)

Figure 126. *PTs 75* and *76* during the assembly phase. These hulls, while being stubbier then other designs, had a sharp hard chined V bottom. The hull was a stepless type with its sides flaring out from the chine to the gunwale, with a flushed deck. (Navy Archives)

Figure 127. A look at *PTs 77, 80, and 82* from the stern. Above decks the Higgins appeared to have a more spacious deck area than the Elco and Huckins designs. The charthouse cabin was small in size and located well forward on the hull. The cockpit, which was just aft of the chartroom, was situated between the two plywood turrets that held the twin .50 calibre machine guns. The engine room took up half the length of the hull, making the crew quarters small and cramped. (Navy Archives)

Figure 128. *PT-87* has been taken to Bayou St. John by rail and awaits her turn to be launched into the water. She sits in her cradle while workers continue to work below decks. No weapons systems have been added yet. (Navy Archives)

78' M.T.B.
QUARTER STERN VIEW
PT 79
CONTRACT NOs. 94729, 94729, EXT 1&2
HIGGINS INDUSTRIES, INC.
NEW ORLEANS, LA., U.S.A.
9-23-42

Figure 129. *PT-78* is in the water waiting for testing. Notice with this design that the boats mufflers are located on the sides of the hull. This early design carries the standard torpedo tubes, using Mk VII or Mk VIII torpedoes. Later, the 200 series Higgins boats would be retrofitted with better torpedoes and light weight racks. These Higgins designed torpedo tubes were powered using compressed air making it difficult for the enemy to spot a fired torpedo, as with the Elco design, which used black powder charges sometimes causing a flash when fired. (Navy Archives)

Figure 130. *PT-80* is warming up her three Packard marine engines as she heads out to Lake Ponchartrain for testing. This boat carries the Oerlikon Mk 4 20mm Cannon on the stern, using the heavier mounted pedestal. This weapon was used primarily in the anti-aircraft role. It was a close range, high angle gun that had a six thousand feet ceiling and a range of five thousand five hundred yards. Because of the design of the two .50 caliber gun turrets (covered with canvas) gunners on board the Higgins boats had a more limited field of fire then the Elco boat. (Author's collection)

Figure 131. During the course of the war, there were many changes to Higgins PT boats. The 200 series sub class boats were retrofitted with the new Mk XIII torpedo and its light weight rack which allowed torpedoes to be rolled off the deck. Type C 300 pound depth charges were added as well. These late war production boats also carried heavier gun armament including a 40 mm Bofors cannon on the stern. 20 mm Mk 4 cannons on a light weight mount were also used on the boats bow section, along with the 37 mm automatic cannon. Radar also made its way onto the boats, giving them an advantage over the enemy. (Alex Johnson)

Figure 132. Another 200 series Higgins boat hull has been completed and will begin another phase of assembly. The Higgins PT boats could turn much quicker and tighter than the Elco boat. One reason can be seen in this photograph. Notice the two large rudders. The Elco boat had three small rudders in their design. This was an important feature of the Higgins boats, as the boats relied heavily on their ability to out maneuver an attacking enemy plane or fast enemy destroyer. (Navy Archives)

Figure 133. A newly designed boat nicknamed the Hellcat was completed in the early summer of 1943. She would undergo builder's trials on June 30, 1943 on Lake Ponchartrain and performed well. The crafts design included a new lower silhouette and offered far greater visibility from the cockpit than earlier models had. At idle speeds the boat threw very little wake, which made it hard to see from the air. The boat reached speeds of fifty-six knots and reversed its course in nine seconds. The Navy would purchase the boat in August, designating it as *PT-564*. Because of the changing demands of the war, the role of the fast torpedo boat had also changed. The PT had become more of a gunboat as enemy surface targets dried up. The Hellcat would not go into production. (Navy Archives)

Figure 134. In 1945, this late-production Higgins boat, *PT-631,* mounted a 37 mm cannon on the bow and two Mk 50 rocket launchers that fired five inch fin-stabilized rockets. The boat saw limited service with Squadron 43, mostly in the training role, before being shipped to the USSR on June 8, 1945. She would be the last class of Higgins PT boats to be constructed during the war. (Author's collection)

Figure 135. A look at one of the late war production Higgins boats. *PT-625* is beginning engine tests and is making her way to Lake Ponchartrain. She carries a 40 mm Bofors cannon on the stern, and her forward machine gun tubs have been moved back from the bridge. She has yet to receive her torpedoes. This boat was placed in service on December 8, 1944 as part of Squadron 43, but was transferred to the USSR on May 22, 1945. (Navy Archives)

Figure 136. *PT-297* running Navy trials in Lake Ponchartrain. Higgins boats were highly maneuverable as can be seen from this photo. The boat carries a 20 mm cannon on the bow as well as one on the stern. Notice the factory applied camouflage on the hull. The SO Radar mast is in the folded position just beyond the helm. This boat later served with Squadron 16B. (Navy Archives)

HUCKINS YACHT CORPORATION

Frank Pembroke Huckins started his Yacht Company in 1928 after selling his family lumber company. His partner was Henry Skinner Baldwin, who took care of the business while Huckins designed and supervised the manufacturing of yachts, which were considered the Duisenberg's of the small-motor yacht class. Huckins was a rugged individualist, a Boston Yankee who had much confidence in his boat-building abilities. Huck actually had his first sail in a rowboat, using an umbrella for power. He was four years old, living in Duxbury, Massachusetts. He later built his first 25 footer in the family barn, cruising around Cape Cod before the canal was built and ran down the Maine coast year after year. That boat—which was whimsically called a submarine because it ran mostly under water—was followed by a whole series of yachts, from his own design.

He built them in his private boathouse in Boston. As the boats grew larger, his cruises reached further until he knew every harbor from Key West to the tip of Newfoundland. His was the first yacht to visit the French Atlantic possession of St. Pierre, where he was taken for a spy enforcing Prohibition and narrowly escaped being bumped off. At length, he became inflamed with the idea that a seagoing yacht could be made to plane and yet not pound, that she would make higher speed on less fuel consumption and ride more steadily Huck decided to move his boat building efforts to Jacksonville, Florida, an ideal place to build boats. Here, he created a wonderfully equipped plant and built a test boat from the hundreds of line drawings he had created over the past six years. The boat began her maiden voyage at night, cruising into the teeth of a rising tropical hurricane. She was driven as far as Bar Harbor, some 1,200 miles, wearing out a number of crews, but not the boat. She planed wonderfully she didn't pound and she was very fast, with low fuel consumption. Otherwise, the boat was terrible. She squirted spray aboard like a snow plow; she would broach, come around and kiss you in a following sea like nobody's business. But Huck had gotten the major qualities he was after. He quickly eliminated the broach and gradually made them drier as each succeeding model appeared. A few years earlier, Huck had integrated his "Huckins System of Quadraconic Projection". This was a very secret mathematical system of unerringly generating the form of hull. This enabled Huckins to create a hull of any size retaining identical characteristics whereby speed, power, and fuel consumption were accurately known beforehand. With the problem of hulls behind him, Huckins attacked mechanisms.

Just about every fitting was made at the Huckins Plant, especially adapted to a particular model, with attention to detail and elimination of annoyances carried to the limit. His first patented invention was the Fairform Leak Alarm, which loudly signaled the bridge, if fuel escaped from anywhere on the boat, thus obviating the cause of fire. He had a series of compact electric pumps, with interchangeable parts that were quiet, used little current, and required little attention, to provide the running water that flushed the Fairform electric toilet and to pump the bilge. To take the backlash out of the steering gear, Huck developed the Fairform Tensioner. His precision controls were well named and permitted accurate handling of a very lively boat. To put twin screw motors in perfect step, he developed the Fairform Synchronizer, and for mileage, the Fairform Recording Log-mechanisms the size of a small alarm clock. Even the lighting fixtures on the Huckins boats were of his own design and manufacture.

Huck stressed the importance of structural members. He maintained that every ounce of weight not necessary to strength and endurance costs money to run and makes a boat labor in heavy seas. His patented laminated keel, which caused much discussion, stood the test of years, running some 600,000 miles and banging against many a rock without failure. These boats in fact were totally laminated. There were five ply watertight bulkheads in some of the larger models, so that even when flooded they could still run many miles with the aft deck nearly awash.

As a result of Huckins's hard work and his devotion to the drawing board, he eventually came out with a complete line of sixteen models, covering every conceivable requirement in a cabin boat. They were all twin screw craft.

Huckins boats were built so well that not once during the great Depression was his plant closed down for lack of orders, a true testament to his design skills Huckins's entry into the PT boat development program came after initial efforts had been made by various boat builders to construct a PT boat that would satisfy the Navy's varied requirements. Twenty PT's were in service and others building before Frank Huckins secured a meeting with Admiral James M. Irish (then a Captain in the Navy Bureau of Ships)

With the world of boat building rather small, it was not surprising that Frank Huckins learned that the boats presently in service were having many problems. He reasoned that with the experience of Huckins in the 1920's and 1930's in building the "fastest seagoing boats in the world," he could build a fast PT boat, and also provide a platform for the armament of such a boat. He told the Navy that he could build a boat that would not pound the teeth out of its crew. Most important to the Navy was that Huckins was willing to spend his own money on such a design. Engines were a problem for Huckins, and he asked the Navy to supply the engines for the boats. The Navy agreed to do so, and Huckins went to work.

At his boat yard in Jacksonville, Florida, Huck went to work. He locked himself in his laboratory, neglected his family, cut his friends, and put in roughly 100 hours a week on the drawing board. He was literally building from the ground up. "We knew that we could do it, but we also knew it would take a little time and patience on our part," he recalled in July of 1941.

Huck's devotion to the program paid off. He came up with a brilliant design he called *PT-69*, a seventy-two foot boat powered by four Packard marine engines. This sleek and fast torpedo boat design met or exceeded the Navy's requirements. It was smaller than the Elco or Higgins designed boats, but its specifications were technologically advanced.

The boat carried two torpedo tubes and had a stern gangway for depth charges. The Huckins Quadraconic hull would prove beneficial. The Navy liked Huckin's small boat design for certain applications. At the time, this class of navy vessel was revolutionary in that it was lightweight and constructed of many types of wood, which made it the fastest boat on the sea. It could race into torpedo range while presenting a low radar profile, fire its torpedoes at the enemy vessel and get away before the enemy could respond.

The Navy trials were scheduled for July 21, 1941, an event which became known as the Plywood Derbies. This was a 190 mile off-shore run to test the boats in an extended run in various sea conditions. *PT-69* fared very well from these sea trials, actually edging out the Elco boats in speed, turning circle, and pounding factor.

In the fall of 1941, the Office of the Chief of Naval Operations and BuShips decided to once again increase the required size of the boats to between 75 and 82 feet. The hull shape would be the hard chine, stepless bottom type with special attention given to minimizing hull stress and fatigue on the crews under all conditions. The boats were to be powered by three Packard marine engines, sustain a speed of 40 knots for one hour, and have a cruising range of at least 500 miles.

Shortly after the specs were provided, Huckins received a contract for eight boats. In July and August of 1942, Huckins delivered his new design, *PTs 95* through *97*, to Squadron 4 at the Motor Torpedo Boat Squadrons Training Center in Melville, Rhode Island. These were the first of the Huckins seventy-eight-foot boats. The remaining boats, *PTs 98* through *102*, were commissioned at Jacksonville Florida and assigned to Squadron 14 at the Panama Sea Frontier. These five boats were later transferred to Squadron 4 for use as training boats. John F. Kennedy commanded *PT- 101* while at the training base for a short time before being transferred to the South Pacific.

Huckins only built ten more boats during the war. They were *PTs 255* through *264*, with Squadron 26, assigned to the Hawaiian Sea Frontier. This squadron was commissioned on March 3, 1943. Officers and crew of the boats had nothing but praise for the boats, reporting they were built well and did not pound them in rough weather. Because Huckins was a small boat yard, they could not mass produce fast enough, only turning out one boat per month. In the time it took Huckins to produce one boat, both Elco and Higgins could turn out fifteen. This was one of the main reasons why Huckins boats never saw combat during the war. In fact, Squadron 15, made up of Higgins boats, was the unit originally scheduled to go to the Hawaiian Sea Frontier, but its orders were changed when two of its divisions were on their way to Panama, and it became the first PT boat squadron sent to the Mediterranean Theater. Simply put, the Higgins boats were ready first.

This was the end of PT boat construction at Huckins; however they did receive a contract from the United States Navy. Contract NObs 1349 called for them to build Hulls #133-165 as 63' Air Sea Rescue Boats, and Hulls #166-169 as seventy-two footers of the same class. After the war, Huckins satisfied a new generation of yachtsmen with a line of performance cruisers. The return from the war of so many men who had been at sea was great for the boat business, and Huck wasted little time in working his magic. He put together a management team that ran Huckins for years to come and on June 13, 1946, launched his third Fairform Flyer. This was the first boat out of the new Huckins plant at the yards current location on the Ortega River.

In May of 1951, Frank Pembroke Huckins died at the age of 65. The man who gave so much of his life to creating first class boats was gone. His designs however, still live forever for future generations to enjoy. Today, some eighty years after Huck started his company; Huckins Yacht Corporation is still in business today, under the direction of his granddaughter, Cindy Purcell. Huckins boats are unmatched for reliability, performance, engineering perfection and style. The small boat yard that produced only eighteen PT boats during the war outlasted both the Elco Naval Division and Higgins Industries. Huckins takes its place in history as possibly the best designed PT boat during the war.

Figure 137. A rare look into the construction of *PT-69*. Workers are busy crawling over the hull of the boat while perched on ladders and wooden scaffolding. Although a small boat yard, Huckins maintained their excellent quality and workmanship throughout the War. This attention to detail and wonderful product would be the main reason Huckins would still be in business some seventy years later. (Huckins Yacht Corporation)

PT95--5 HUCKINS

Figure 138. The inside of the boat shows the engine beds that would accept the Packard marine engines. This close up view shows the engine mounting foundation with shaped longitude stringers. Notice the steel mounting channels and one of the exit ports for one of the propeller shafts. (Huckins Yacht Corporation)

Figure 139. A look at the galley on *PT-69*. To the left is the full sized electric refrigerator. Notice the three burner gas stove, and Chrome Dressler sink, with Drawers and locker below. The water tight door led to the Officers Quarters, with a ladder to topside. (Huckins Yacht Corporation)

Figure 140.Officer's quarters on *PT-69*. This shows the lower bunk set up, with privacy curtain. To the left are the Lockers for storage. This is looking from the galley of the boat. The door with privacy curtain would lead to the sound gear or ammo room heading aft. (Huckins Yacht Corporation)

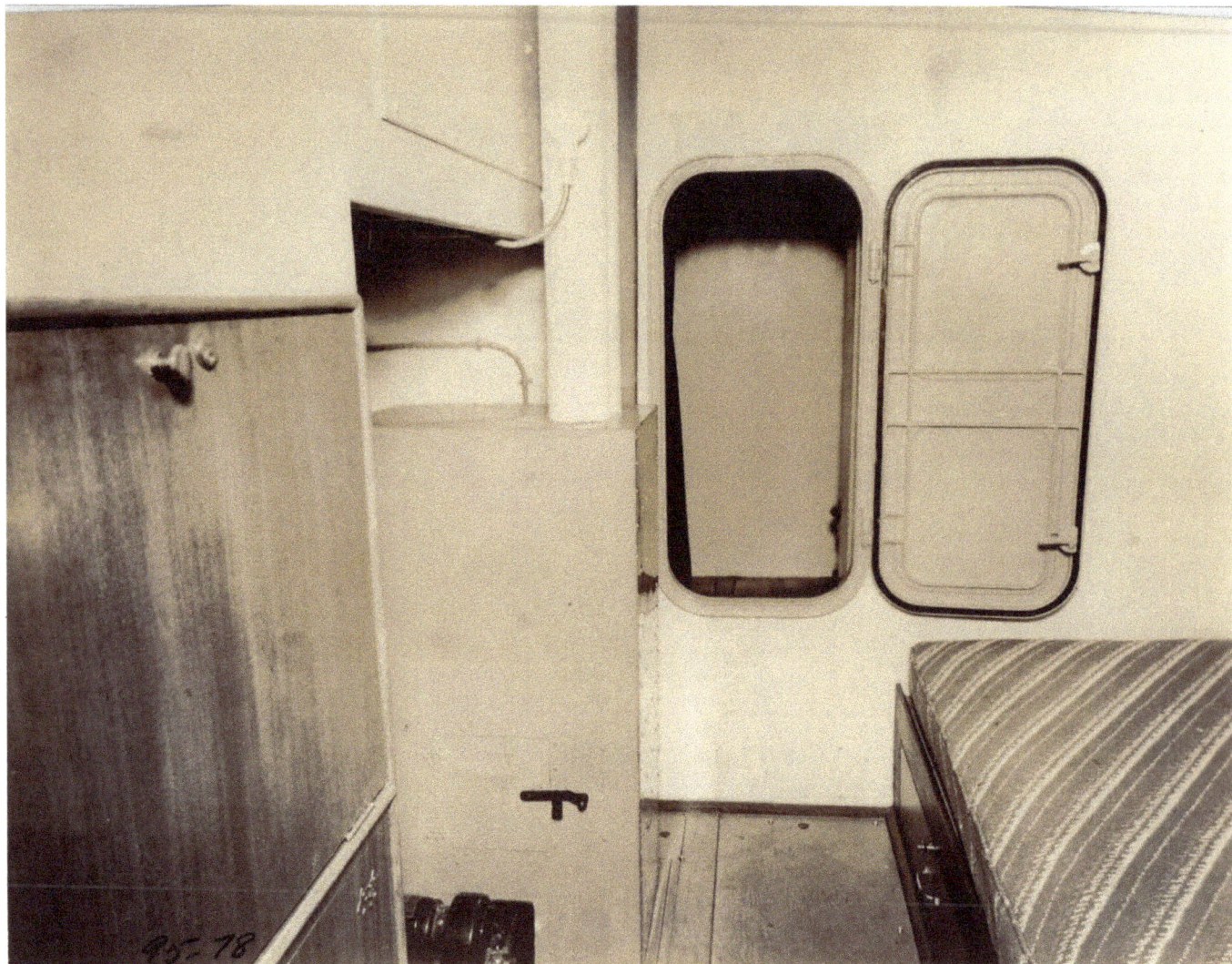

Figure 141. Another look at the officers' quarters showing the large heater installed. The lower bunk also has pull out drawers. Notice again the water tight door, which was not used on the later Huckins boats. The bunks had very comfortable mattresses. (Huckins Yacht Corporation)

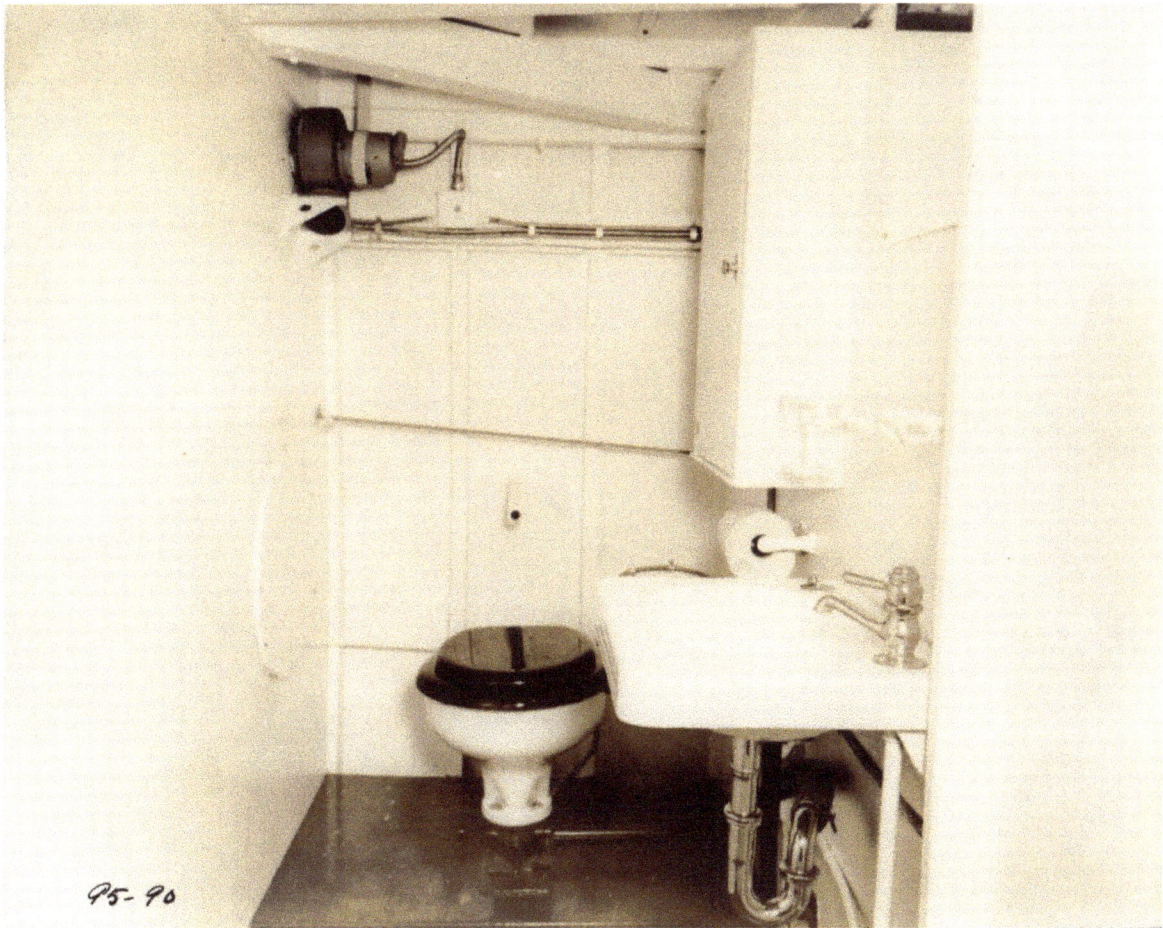

Figure 142. Small but efficient officer's head. A simple toilet, sink, and cabinet were
included. (Huckins Yacht Corporation)

Figure 143. Forward crews quarters on the boat showing the upper and lower berths. Lower bunks contained slide out drawers for the crew, but little in the way of other lockers. Ladder would lead to topside, which had hinged hatches with screens. Just forward of the steps was a 700 gallon fuel tank and small rope locker. (Huckins Yacht Corporation)

Figure 144. Looking aft of the crew's quarters. The water tight door led to the galley with two locker areas to the left and right of the door. (Huckins Yacht Corporation)

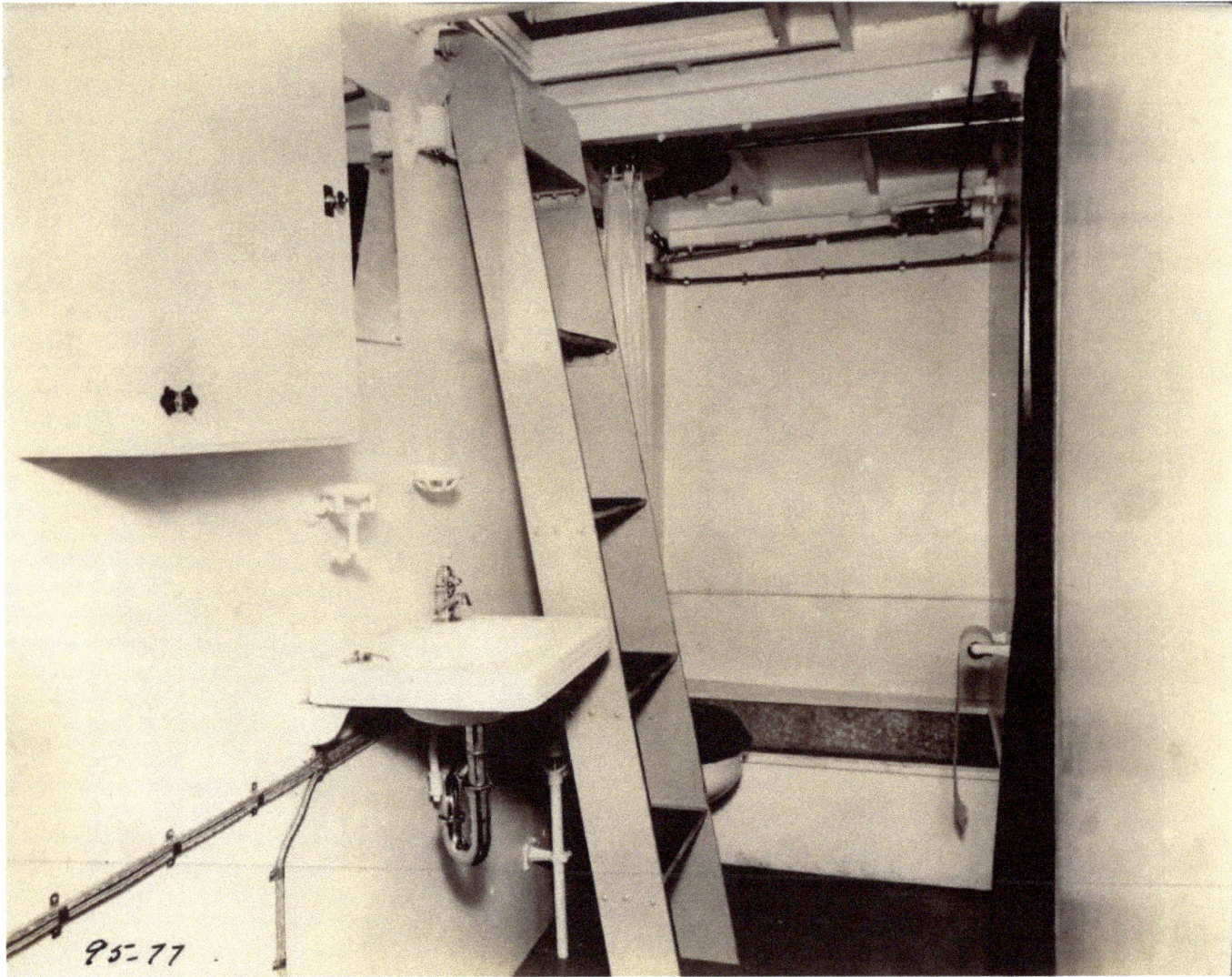

Figure 145. Crew's head complete with toilet (just beyond ladder) sink, and cabinet. The enclosed space also has a shower for the crew (potable water tank 100 gallons). It is unknown as to why the ladder was placed in this already cramped space. (Huckins Yacht Corporation)

Figure 146. The Frank Huckins *PT-69* shown during Sea trials. This seventy-two-foot design would carry four 1,200-hp Packard marine engines. Huckins used his own Quadraconic hull design, which would minimize stress on the hull and fatigue of the crew. She carried two .50 calibre gun tubs, and two 21-inch torpedo tubes. The boat had a stern gangway for depth charges, and four cast steel rudders on the stern, making the boat highly maneuverable. (PT Boats Inc., Germantown, Tennessee)

MT-72-54

Figure 147. Work began on the second production run of Huckins boats shortly after completion of the Plywood Derbies. The CNO and BuShips increased the size of the Huckins boats to seventy-eight feet. The galley remained pretty much the same, except for changes to the stove system and removal of the water tight door. (Huckins Yacht Corporation)

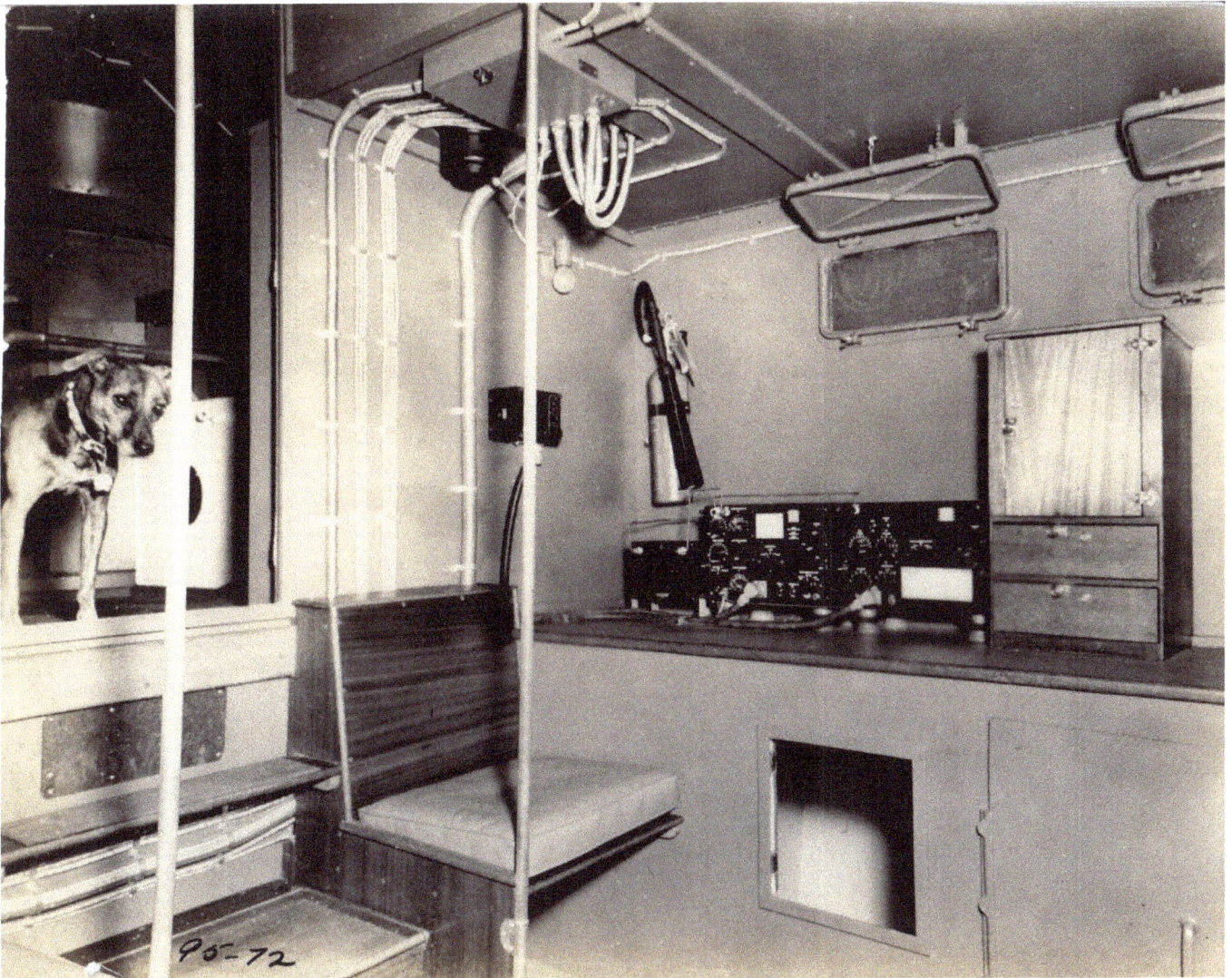

Figure 148. The port side radio room of *PT-95* shows the radioman's seat and radio gear, which include an early TCS short wave radio set. To the left is Fairfa the dog, who is making sure everything is ship shape. Fairfa was Huck's dog that accompanied him everywhere, even to cocktail parties. (Huckins Yacht Corporation)

Figure 149. The engine room with three Packard marine engines (looking forward) shows the extra head room that was available in the Huckins boats. Because of the high freeboard, one could actually stand up. Engineers on the boats could work in relative comfort. The large white boxes over-head are water and oil expansion tanks. The long metal rods are connected to the reverse gear ends of the engines shifting levers, which run to the engineer's station forward. (Huckins Yacht Corporation)

Figure 150. Forward from the engine room, through the water tight door, was the engineer's station. Located on the wall were the electrical read outs for all three engines. Above the panel to the right were the control throttles used in the case of emergencies. Shifting for the engines was done here (shifting D- handles on bulkhead) for forward, neutral or reverse. Notice the small black round clutch handles also on the bulkhead. D-handles connected to the reverse gear units of the engines. (Huckins Yacht Corporation)

Figure 151. The roomy helm area of *PT-95* shows the efficient layout of the controls. To the left are the six gauges for RPM and manifold pressure readouts. To the right, switches and plunger buttons are for alarm, bilge pump, engine, horn, aft horn, search light, and wipers. The skipper and executive officer at the helm were also better protected than on the Elco and Higgins boats from wind and spray, due to the Huckins-designed windshield. The open door was the entry to the forward charthouse cabin. (Huckins Yacht Corporation)

Figure 152. *PT-95* has been launched at Merril Stevens's boat yard in Jacksonville, Florida. This would be Huckins's first seventy-eight-foot design, which was delivered to the Navy's Motor Torpedo Boat Squadrons Training Center. She served with Squadron 4 as a training boat for recruits. The boat still needs to be outfitted with two forward torpedo tubes, .50 calibre Browning machine guns, depth charges, and stern mounted 20 mm cannon. Next to her is *PT-96*, ready for launching. (Huckins Yacht Corporation)

Figure 153. *PT-95* running builder's trials off Jacksonville, Florida on July 4, 1942. Although she did not have the graceful lines of the Elco boats, she had a better turning radius and rode the waves with less pounding then the early Elco PT boats. She now carries all of her armament package available at that time. Huckins designed the hulls to plane on the water, rather then cutting through it like other designs. The boat was placed in service on July 30, 1943.

Figure 154. Frank P. Huckins, the man behind the success of Huckins Yacht Corporation stands in the Helm area of *PT-97*. This seventy-eight-foot boat was delivered to Squadron 4 as a training boat. It would be placed in service on August 29, 1943. Huck smokes his trademark pipe and was not often seen without it. He later claimed that his hull design would save the PT boat from failure. (Huckins Yacht Corporation)

Figure 155. Stern view of *PT-95* shows her three rudders. The part seen above the water line are the guards for the rudder control drive rods. The three rudders of the Huckins boats were small in size, a surprising fact when you consider the tight turning ability of the boat. The smoke generator is on the stern (seen here) along with several empty depth charge racks. (Huckins Yacht Corporation)

H-4

Figure 156. Launched from the Merril Stevens boat yard, these *95*-class Huckins boats seved with Squadron 14. This special ceremony included Navy representatives from the BuShips, yard workers, and invited guests. To the left of the Navy (JG) officer at the microphone is Henry Baldwin (with arms folded in front of him), Huckins's partner. Behind the Officer at the microphone (In white coat/white pants, holding a pipe) is Frank P. Huckins, and to his right (woman shading her eyes) is his wife, Betty. Christening of the boats was usually done by one of the foremen's wives. (Notice the women holding flowers to the left of the officer on the microphone). (Huckins Yacht Corporation)

Figure 157. Three boats that became a part of Squadron 14 tie up at the Mayport Naval Air Station in Jacksonville, Florida. To the left is *PT-101,* and to the right, *PT-98.* The designation of the center boat is unknown. Notice the small U.S. Mail boat from Jacksonville also tied to the pier. The boats carry the 20 mm cannon on the stern, with Mk-XIII torpedoes. Two of the boats do not have their torpedo tubes installed as there was a shortage of the tubes during this time. It is possible that the boats did not receive their torpedoes until reaching the Panama Sea Frontier. (Huckins Yacht Corporation)

Figure 158. *PT*-7 plies the waters in Jacksonville, Florida shortly after being placed in service on August 29, 1943. This boat became a part of Squadron 4 at the Motor Torpedo Boat Squadrons Training Center at Melville, Rhode Island. (PT Boats Inc., Germantown, Tennessee)

1.

Figure 159. The second production runs of Huckins PT boats were numbered 255 through 264. Changes to these boats were increased engine horsepower, a newly designed system that replaced the earlier windshield and of course increased armament. These boats would be assigned to Squadron 26 as part of the Hawaiian Sea Frontier. Here we see *PT-264* running Navy Trials, shortly before being placed in service on September 7, 1943. (Huckins Yacht Corporation)

Figure 160. *PT-262* jumps the waves showing her beautifully designed hull. She carries the SO radar dome, with two Mk-XIII torpedoes in roll off racks. She also carries a 37 mm automatic cannon on the Bow. Assigned to Squadron 26, these boats relieved Squadron One at Pearl Harbor, based at Pearl City Yacht Club. *PTs 255-258* were ordered to Midway to replace other boats, becoming the defense force at Midway Island, along with an old four-stack destroyer, long after the battle of Midway was over. (Huckins Yacht Corporation)

Figure 161. Another look at *PT-262* as she produces a powerful wake. The boat is near her top speed with all those on hand holding on. These wakes, although wonderful, could be spotted easily from the air by enemy planes. Engineers worked throughout the war to try and minimize this effect with few results. The boat carries the 40 mm Bofors Cannon on the stern. (Huckins Yacht Corporation)

Figure 162. Squadron 26 boats make a beautiful picture as they head out for patrol in
Hawaii. The boats were used for ready-boat duty, monitoring the radio on a twenty-
four hour basis, looking for downed flyers. The boats also conducted training
exercises outside of Pearl Harbor, conducting mock torpedo attacks as our Navy
ships would come out. The boats, standing by on the southwest corner of Maui at
sundown, would try to sneak in. If undetected, the boats would continue to move
in, but if spotted the ships would fire star shells, telling the boats to withdraw.
(Huckins Yacht Corporation)

Figure 163. The author was invited to visit the old Elco Naval Division site in 1998. What he found was the remains of building 21 and the original dockside crane. Years of neglect had taken their toll as evident from this photo. Notice that the concrete roadway has buckled and fallen into the basin. The crane was still in operation and was used for pleasure craft. A sad ending for such a historic place. Later another fire completely destroyed building 21, but the crane was dismantled and stored away. Thanks to Baker Residential, which developed the old Elco site, the crane was preserved and the structure fully restored. In 2006, the crane was reassembled in Rutkowski Park at the North West side of Bayonne's Hudson County Park. Once more the crane proudly stands not far from where she once guided PT boats into Newark Bay.

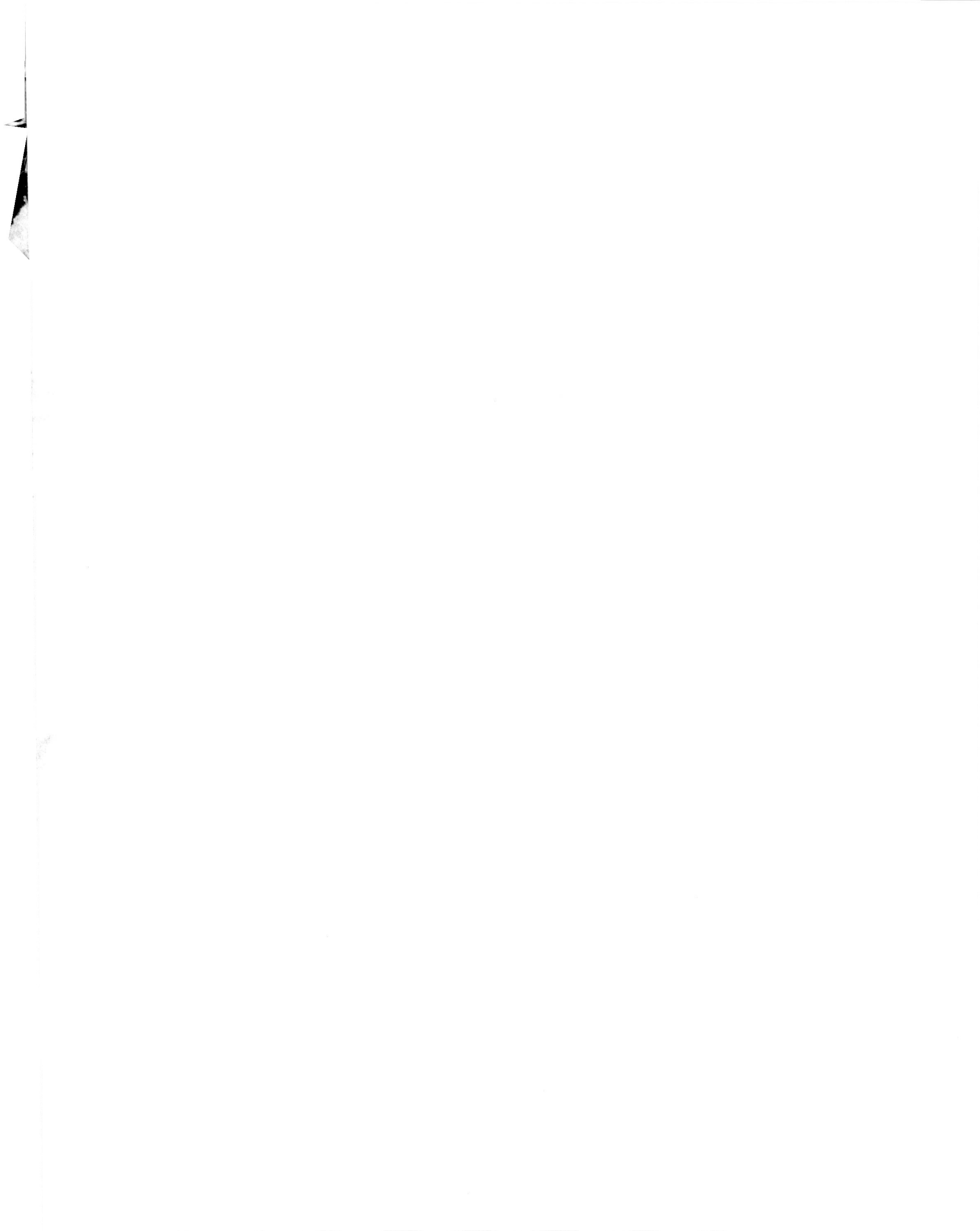

www.ingramcontent.com/pod-product-compliance
Lightning Source LLC
Chambersburg PA
CBHW061231150426

42812CB00054BA/2560

9 781608 880737